EPIC ATHLETES
KEVIN DURANT

Dan Wetzel
Illustrations by Marcelo Baez

Henry Holt and Company
New York

Henry Holt and Company, *Publishers since 1866*
Henry Holt® is a registered trademark of Macmillan Publishing Group, LLC
120 Broadway, New York, NY 10271 • mackids.com

Library of Congress Cataloging-in-Publication Data
Names: Wetzel, Dan, author. | Baez, Marcelo, illustrator.
Title: Kevin Durant / Dan Wetzel ; Illustrations by Marcelo Baez.
Description: First edition. | New York : Henry Holt and Company, [2020] |
Series: Epic athletes; 8 | Includes bibliographical references. | Summary:
"The eighth book in a middle-grade nonfiction sports series that focuses on
today's superstars and up-and-comers"—Provided by publisher.
Identifiers: LCCN 2019040937 | ISBN 9781250295835 (hardcover)
Subjects: LCSH: Durant, Kevin, 1988– | Basketball players—
United States—Biography—Juvenile literature.
Classification: LCC GV884.D868 W48 2020 | DDC 796.323092 [B]—dc23
LC record available at https://lccn.loc.gov/2019040937

Our books may be purchased in bulk for promotional, educational, or business use.
Please contact your local bookseller or the Macmillan Corporate
and Premium Sales Department at (800) 221-7945 ext. 5442 or
by email at MacmillanSpecialMarkets@macmillan.com.

First edition, 2020 / Designed by Elynn Cohen
Printed in the United States of America
by LSC Communications, Harrisonburg, Virginia
1 3 5 7 9 10 8 6 4 2

Also by Dan Wetzel

Epic Athletes
STEPHEN CURRY

Epic Athletes
ALEX MORGAN

Epic Athletes
TOM BRADY

Epic Athletes
SERENA WILLIAMS

Epic Athletes
LEBRON JAMES

Epic Athletes
LIONEL MESSI

1

The Shot

IT WAS THE FINAL MINUTE of the fourth quarter of Game 3 of the 2017 National Basketball Association (NBA) Finals and a single basket—or rebound, steal, missed shot, or turnover—by either team could swing not just this neck-and-neck contest, but potentially the entire championship. The Cleveland Cavaliers led the Golden State Warriors, 113–111 in a matchup that was about as close and tense as basketball can get.

Golden State had jumped to a 2–0 lead in the best-of-seven Finals, but heading into this contest, the Warriors knew better than to get overconfident. Just a year prior they'd won seventy-three regular season games and led these same Cavs 3–1 in The Finals. They'd looked like one of the greatest teams in NBA history. Then LeBron James led a historic comeback that saw Cleveland win Games 5, 6, and 7 and take the NBA championship.

Now a year later, late in Game 3, every single Warriors player, coach, and fan had to wonder if LeBron might do enough to win this game and steal another championship from Golden State.

That's when Kevin Durant reached up high with his long, long right arm and snatched a missed Cleveland shot out of the air. Suddenly Golden State was on the offensive with a chance to tie—or take the lead.

Moments like this were exactly why the Warriors had brought Kevin to the team. And this was exactly the type of moment Kevin had hoped would come when he'd signed with Golden State. He hadn't played for the Warriors in 2015–16 when they'd fallen short of winning The Finals. In the offseason that followed, Golden State signed Kevin as a free agent because the team felt it lacked one more player who could come up big in the sport's loneliest of moments—when the pressure of roaring fans and high stakes cause nerves to fray. They felt they needed someone who could close out games, like tonight, and thus would ensure that another LeBron-style comeback never happened again.

Officially Kevin is listed at six foot nine, but he's admitted that in his signature Nikes, he stands seven feet tall. He said he likes being listed as shorter than his true height as a joke, part of his fun, free-spirited personality.

He'd always been the tallest anyway—the tallest in his class in kindergarten, fourth grade, and middle school. He was this skinny kid who kept growing and growing and growing while being raised in Prince George's County, Maryland, just outside of Washington, DC. As much as his height helped him become a talented basketball player, it was his arms that set him apart even in the NBA, where almost everyone is tall.

With his arms stretched out, Kevin's wingspan measured seven foot five end to end, and somehow he was still coordinated. He could shoot and dribble like someone a foot shorter. Yet he could rebound and block shots in a way no six-foot guard could even dream of doing.

So snagging that rebound was the easy part. What to do next was the tougher decision.

There were about fifty-one seconds remaining in the game. Golden State needed a basket. It needed a hero.

Kevin had always felt he was built for these kinds of make-or-break scenarios. His combination of size and skill made him nearly impossible to defend. He felt that when his team needed to score, he was the one capable of doing it, especially in big games.

Yet getting to the ultimate pressure-filled stage, The Finals, had proven difficult for him throughout his career. He'd spent eight years playing for the Oklahoma City Thunder (and one year prior when the team had been based in Seattle and was called the SuperSonics). He'd reached one NBA Finals in 2012, but lost to LeBron, who was playing for Miami then.

Kevin was twenty-two years old at the time and thought he'd return regularly to The Finals.

He didn't. Oklahoma City always fell short. Sometimes it was in the Western Conference Finals. Sometimes it was due to injury. Whatever it was, Kevin couldn't get the NBA championship that he coveted.

He noted that he'd spent his entire basketball life in second place. He'd been ranked the number two high school player in the country. He was the number two pick in the 2007 NBA draft. He finished, for years, at number two in the NBA's MVP voting (although he eventually won the award in 2014). He was always the runner-up, and never the champion. After ten years in the league, he'd made millions of dollars and acquired millions of fans, he'd starred in movies and television commercials, he was huge on social media, and he had become active in charitable giving.

The one thing he didn't have, however, was an NBA title.

He wanted one so desperately that he left Oklahoma City, where he was a beloved fan favorite and life was comfortable, to join the powerhouse Warriors in Oakland, where he needed to adjust his game and mentality to fit in with other established players. At Golden State, he wouldn't be the most popular player (that was Steph Curry), but he thrived on being part of a true team that could win it all.

So now he had not just the ball in his hand but destiny as well. Over twenty thousand Cavaliers fans were beginning to shout inside of the Quicken Loans

Arena in downtown Cleveland, screaming to distract Kevin as he took the ball and began dribbling it up the court. "De-fense!" they chanted. "De-fense!"

That Kevin was able to masterfully handle the ball, at such a height, was a wonder that had become commonplace. He made it look easy, but in the rich history of basketball, there may never have been a player this tall who could dribble so well. There may never have been a seven-footer who could so effortlessly take over the role of point guard in an instant.

It had begun back in Prince George's County, at a simple city recreational building in his hometown of Seat Pleasant. It was in Seat Pleasant that Kevin grew up with his older brother, Tony, raised mostly by his mother and grandmother (his father would reenter his life later). It was there that he met a couple of youth basketball coaches, Taras Brown and Charles Craig.

While they saw a kid who was taller than the other players, they didn't teach him the game in the traditional way. They didn't want Kevin to just play down low and grab rebounds, or learn only to score around the basket, as is the case for most power forwards and centers. He was too athletically gifted for that and his coaches saw that the sport of basketball was changing.

They taught Kevin how to play all the positions, including schooling him on dribbling, passing, and shooting from a distance by putting him through endless, repetitive drills. Dribbling through cones. Dribbling with both hands. Dribbling two balls at once. Dribbling, dribbling, dribbling.

Then they'd move on to shooting practice. Shot after shot, day after day, year after year. It was a basketball science project, like they were creating the perfect player in a lab. And Kevin was all for it, a tireless worker who understood that there were no shortcuts to becoming truly great.

Each repetition slowly caused his muscles to memorize the kind of form and touch that would never abandon him—even when his team needed a basket and he knew it wasn't just all those Cleveland fans watching him, but the entire basketball world.

As Kevin pulled that rebound out of the air and brought it down to his body, he spun his head and saw open space in front of him. The Cavaliers were charging back to play defense, to guard against the Warriors whipsaw offense that called for players to dart in all directions until someone got open. It might be Steph Curry, the two-time MVP. It might be Klay Thompson, the clutch three-point specialist. It might go down low to Draymond Green, who could power home a bucket.

No one knew at the moment that Kevin Durant, who had worked and waited his entire life for this chance, wasn't going to pass it to anyone. He thought back to his earliest days in the game, playing as a kid on a local Amateur Athletic Union (AAU) team, and knew what was expected of him.

"Every team I'm on, in order for us to go to the next level, I have to assert myself," Kevin said. "Since I was playing for the [Prince George's] Jaguars when I was ten years old, I felt like if I didn't assert myself, we weren't as good as we should be."

Which was just fine with his teammates.

"We know in that situation to get that man the rock," Klay Thompson said. "He's seven foot, can shoot over almost anybody, and has amazing shooting touch."

With a single focus in mind, Kevin started up the court, his long strides covering huge swaths of hardwood. One dribble. Two dribbles. No one from Cleveland rushed up to stop him. A third dribble and he was now past the half-court line.

LeBron was waiting at the three-point line, but was slowly retreating, giving Kevin more room. Clearly LeBron thought Kevin, with his team down two points, would drive to the hoop and try to tie the game. Kevin had other ideas.

"I [saw] him backing up and I just wanted to take that shot," Kevin said.

He took a fourth dribble and casually slowed his run, as if he were about to stop and set up the offense. It was enough for LeBron to relax, ever so slightly. Yet when Kevin approached the three-point line, he didn't stop and look to pass, he just set his size eighteen Nikes down twenty-six feet from the basket and pulled up to shoot.

LeBron, a beat too late, tried to react and leaped at Kevin with an outstretched arm that sought to at least harass Kevin into a miss. Kevin didn't even notice. His jumper was so smooth, so textbook, he just rose and fired.

"I just tried to stay disciplined in my shot, hold my follow-through," Kevin said.

The ball soared toward the hoop in a perfect arc. *Swish.*

It was the shot of a lifetime after a lifetime of making shots.

"Durant from three!" said the announcer on ESPN. "It's good. Kevin Durant from downtown as Golden State takes the lead."

Warriors 114. Cavaliers 113.

"KD said, 'I've been working on that shot my entire life,'" Steph Curry said after. "Literally that's his mindset—'I'm ready to take this shot because I haven't cheated the game. I put the time in every year to get better . . . and to be ready for those kind of moments.'"

Seconds later Cleveland's Kyrie Irving would miss a shot. Then Kevin would get fouled and sent to the line, where he made both free throws to extend the Warriors' lead. Cleveland missed again and then Steph salted away the game when he hit two more free throws.

Golden State celebrated a 118–113 victory and a commanding 3–0 lead in the NBA Finals.

Two games later, they closed the series out and Kevin Durant became a champion, at last. He was named NBA Finals MVP. He was no longer second best at anything.

"It feels," Kevin said after, "so great."

2
Early Years

KEVIN WAYNE DURANT was born September 29, 1988, in Suitland, Maryland, just outside of Washington, DC. His parents were Wanda and Wayne Pratt. Kevin was the family's second child, joining his brother, Anthony ("Tony"), who was about three years older.

Kevin's parents were just twenty-one years old when they had him, and the stress of a growing family weighed on his father. Within a year of Kevin's birth, Wayne Pratt separated from his wife and kids, leaving Wanda alone as a single mother. She was forced to make ends meet and raise two active, growing boys on her own.

"I was immature, selfish, I was young," Kevin's dad would tell the *Washington Post* years later. "I didn't know what I was getting myself into."

Kevin's mother was also young, but she didn't have a choice in what to do. She divorced Wayne, and Tony and Kevin took her maiden name, Durant, as their last name. Wanda worked a series of jobs in an attempt to pay rent and feed her kids.

While Seat Pleasant sits just seven or so miles from the White House, it is not a wealthy or fancy neighborhood. It is a small, working-class suburb, filled with mostly African American families that take pride in their community and helping their children achieve their potential.

At times Kevin and his family lived with his grandmother, Barbara Davis. She owned a small yellow house with a front porch on a corner lot in Seat Pleasant. It wasn't much, but it was everything to Kevin and Tony—out back there was a field to play in and in the kitchen there was always a hot meal being prepared. Grandma helped raise the kids when they lived in her house and their mother was at work.

While the family loved Grandma's house, it was

too small for four people. Kevin, his mom, and his brother moved often, always looking for an apartment they could stay in long-term. That meant Kevin and Tony had to keep switching schools and making new friends. Money was extremely tight. Kevin's mom worked just to get by, often skipping meals or wearing old dresses so she could instead feed and clothe her boys. Every day felt like a struggle.

"The odds were stacked against us," Kevin said. "Single parent with two boys."

"I didn't make a lot of money," Wanda Pratt told ABC-TV years later. "I was twenty-one with two small children. I had to figure out how we were going to do this, how we were going to make it. I decided early on that my desires and wants and even needs came second to what they needed and wanted. That was my mindset."

She eventually got a steady job with the United States Postal Service that paid well enough for the family to get its own apartment in Seat Pleasant. At last they would have a place of their own to return to day after day, including rooms where they could hang posters on the walls and neighborhood kids they could befriend without fear of moving in a few months.

"One of the best memories I had was when we moved into our first apartment," Kevin recalled. "No bed, no furniture and we just sat in the living room and just hugged each other. We thought we made it."

Kevin's grandmother remained heavily involved in the boys' lives, often picking them up from school, fixing peanut butter and jelly sandwiches for them, and helping with homework when Wanda had to work late. On Sundays, the extended family would gather at Grandma's house for big dinners. Even with his father gone, Kevin didn't lack for discipline or stability in his family. Not with his loving mother and grandmother around.

As early as anyone could remember, Kevin was tall for his age. Even before he reached kindergarten, he sprung up above everyone else and remained there, this long, skinny kid who just kept getting longer and skinnier. This wasn't a surprise since both of Kevin's parents were tall—his dad stood six-three and his mother six-foot. Tony was big, too—he'd eventually reach six foot seven. But Kevin was the tallest, and although his height would come to help him later in life, as a child he was often embarrassed by the attention.

Other kids would tease him. Adults would see his height and assume he was a couple years older than he was and then wonder why he acted or spoke the way he did. Kevin might have looked nine, but he was actually only six, and there is a big difference between the maturity levels of a six- and nine-year-old. Sometimes his arms were so long for his body that he had trouble with his coordination. At an age when kids want to fit in, there was no way for Kevin to avoid standing out. It sometimes caused him to be shy.

Kevin's family tried to teach him to be proud of his size and not worry what everyone else said. One school year, Kevin had a teacher who would line the students up from shortest to tallest before marching through the hallways of the elementary school. Kevin's mother asked her to change that process and sometimes go in reverse order, tallest to shortest, so her son wouldn't feel like he was always last in line and somehow take that to believe he was inferior.

The one area where his size helped him was in sports. Kevin was always playing some game, usually because he was following his older brother. Tony was a good athlete and whatever Tony was doing, Kevin was usually right behind him. "I always wanted to follow in [his] footsteps," Kevin said. Besides, it seemed like every kid in their neighborhood played football, basketball, or just about anything else they could. Sometimes it was down at the park. Sometimes it was out in the street. It didn't matter. If there was a ball, someone was running with it, dribbling it, shooting it.

When Kevin was eight, he signed up to play basketball at the local Seat Pleasant Activity Center. Basketball, everyone said, was where his height would be a positive, not something to be ashamed about.

Around that time, he met two basketball coaches. One, Charles "Chucky" Craig, ran the activity center and coached the young kids who came to play basketball. The other, Taras Brown, worked not just with kids at the center, but also ran a local travel basketball team.

Kevin and Coach Craig hit it off right away. Coach Craig later described Kevin as a "want-to-player," a kid with the drive and desire to be great who was willing to do whatever it took to get there. Even at a young age, he was as interested in working on fundamentals such as dribbling, passing, and shooting as he was in playing games. That, as much as his height, made Kevin special.

Kevin was at the rec center all the time. He'd go there after school and play basketball. He'd spend weekends there. He was always looking to work out. Kevin quickly became obsessed with basketball. His mother recalls walking into the living room once and seeing Kevin playing with some Matchbox cars, but rather than racing them around the room, he had them positioned and was moving them slowly. She was confused.

"I said, 'Kevin, what are you doing with those,'" Wanda Pratt told reporters. "And he said, 'Mom, I'm just coming up with basketball plays.' So he was dedicated early on as a kid to basketball."

Coach Craig saw a kid with a lot of potential who needed to learn the basics. They became more than just coach and player—Coach Craig served as a father figure to Kevin and they were always together.

"It was days where I spent the whole day with him," Kevin told *The Oklahoman* newspaper.

Coach Brown saw the same spark of talent in Kevin. It wasn't just Kevin's size and ability that drew the coaches to him. It was his attitude. He was always listening and was eager to please.

"At a young age he never wanted to disappoint anybody," Coach Brown told the *Warriors Huddle* podcast. "He did whatever you asked of him. He also had a way of making everyone around him feel good . . . He also wanted to know what he could do better. He was always concerned with working hard."

As Kevin progressed as a player, Coach Brown pushed him harder and harder. Through the years, Coach Brown has helped develop numerous college and NBA players, and he believed that the lessons learned early are the keys to success. Coach Brown thought Kevin had not only the natural ability, but also the dedication to become an NBA player. Every day was considered one more step in that ultimate direction.

Since Kevin was so tall for his age, and doctors believed he would continue to grow, many coaches thought Kevin should play the center position. While Kevin was growing up during the 1990s and 2000s, many of the best players in the NBA were big, tall centers—Shaquille O'Neal, Yao Ming, Hakeem Olajuwon, Alonzo Mourning, Tim Duncan, and others. They often stood over seven feet tall.

Those players tended to play as close to the basket as possible. Using their height, they blocked shots and grabbed rebounds. They scored most of their points by setting up with their back to the basket, close to the hoop on what is often called the "low post," and then spinning or maneuvering a short distance for a layup or dunk.

But Coach Brown thought Kevin was a different type of player. Kevin was a guy who could play near the basket, but also out on the perimeter, where he'd shoot jump shots, handle the ball, and run the floor. For a player his size, Kevin had a surprisingly good shot.

"It may have been the ugliest shot you've ever seen, but it went in," Coach Brown said. "So all I had to do was fine-tune it."

Coach Brown made Kevin study some of the new wave of NBA big men who played facing the basket. He told him to study their moves and read articles on them. He also turned to a retired star, Larry Bird, who in the 1980s had been named the NBA's Most Valuable Player three times and led the Boston Celtics to three NBA championships.

Larry was six foot nine, but at a time when many players that size were told to play close to the basket, he excelled at shooting three-pointers. Larry had grown up in a small town in Indiana, also mostly without a father, and he passed a lot of time practicing by himself, slowly getting better and better at hitting shots from farther and farther away.

The hoop was the one constant in Larry's life, the one place he could always turn even when his home life was difficult. Kevin felt the same way, and his work ethic was very similar to Larry's. By the time Larry made the NBA, he was a trailblazer. He played on the perimeter, not down near the hoop. His height made his shot almost impossible to block, and he became one of the greatest players of all time.

Coach Brown figured Kevin would grow around as tall, if not taller, than Larry, so if he could duplicate that shot, it would push Kevin to the NBA.

"I told him early on, you're not going to be a center and we are going to work on your perimeter skills," Coach Brown said on the *Warriors Huddle* podcast.

Kevin, watching video after video of Larry playing basketball, agreed. It all made sense.

"He allowed players like myself to kind of dream big and think big at that position," Kevin said. "And to do things that traditional small forwards or big men weren't doing."

To help with his development, Coach Brown

would make Kevin lie on his back and flick a weighted medicine ball up in the air, mimicking a jump shot. That helped him build strength in his wrists. He told Kevin to take what felt like endless shots and kept a close eye on his form and the placement of the elbow on his shooting hand. Kevin also did lots and lots of push-ups.

Coach Brown believed in the simplicity of the game. At Kevin's height, you didn't need a million moves to be able to score. You just needed a couple, but you needed to do them perfectly. So he made Kevin practice them over and over and over.

"I told him, 'I am going to teach you three moves and if you can do those three moves you'll be successful,'" Coach Brown said on the podcast.

Kevin Durant, always willing to learn and never wanting to disappoint, was all in.

3

Climbing High

NOT FAR FROM THE Seat Pleasant Activity Center sits the corner of L Street and Balsamtree Drive. It's a typical intersection in the middle of a residential neighborhood, surrounded mostly by houses. It was a place Kevin dreaded to visit, but he also appreciated what it represented.

From that corner, L Street begins a steep incline into what is called "Hunt's Hill" or just "the Hill." It isn't very long, but it climbs so quickly, and so high up, that from the top, if the weather is clear, you can see all the way into Washington, DC.

Almost every day after practice, Coach Brown would take Kevin over to the base of the Hill and point up L Street. He'd then order Kevin to sprint to its top, as fast as he could. It was a brutal exercise, the kind that causes leg muscles to burn and make lungs feel like they are about to collapse. Once at the top, Kevin had to immediately backpedal down. While going downhill is normally easier, Kevin was tasked with moving in the way basketball players often do when getting back on defense. When that was done, he had to do it again. And again. Typically, he completed a set of twenty-five before Coach Brown was satisfied.

Sometimes Kevin's mother would come by and park her car at the bottom of the Hill, waiting for Kevin to finish up so she could drive him home for dinner. For Wanda, this was a rare moment for herself, without the demands of either work or home. She used the time to read a book and occasionally, if she was enjoying what she was reading, she'd make Kevin do an extra twenty-five sprints up and back-pedals down the Hill just so she could finish her chapter.

The runs were tough, but that was the point. Coach Brown figured that if Kevin could develop the endurance necessary to run up the Hill, which is a few basketball courts long, then he'd never get tired in an actual game. This was about more than just conditioning, though. This was also about toughness, both mental and physical. Sprinting up the Hill was a challenge, something that no one wanted to do. If Kevin could do it, then he would begin to believe he could power through any obstacle.

Kevin agreed. "I knew that it would make me better," he told reporters years later while on a tour of his old neighborhood. "I really just did anything that he told me to do. I had to if I wanted to get better. I hated it at the time, but I knew it would make me better in the long run. It built up that work ethic and that discipline."

During the summers, Kevin became a regular at the Seat Pleasant Activity Center. Kevin often got there so early that he'd have to wait outside until ten a.m. when it opened. He would then stay until it closed at five p.m. After a two-hour break, the center would reopen at seven p.m. for evening hours. There were times Kevin didn't want to have to trudge all the way back to his grandmother's home, about ten minutes away, for such a brief amount of time.

He took notice of a big curtain that hung on one

side of the gym and realized it was rare for anyone to go back there. One day, Kevin decided to sneak behind it just before the five p.m. closing. Since no one noticed he was there, he stayed at the Activity Center until it reopened two hours later.

When he quietly emerged around seven, he went undetected by any of the staff. With his plan a success, that nook soon became his secret hiding spot so he could stay at the gym all day long. Sometimes he'd take naps. Sometimes he'd just lie there and think.

"When the rec center was closed, I would sit behind that curtain and go to sleep on a mat, like a yoga mat almost," Kevin told reporters. "I spent, literally, all my time there every day. And it paid off."

Coach Brown and Coach Craig didn't just coach at the activity center, they also ran a travel basketball team called the PG Jaguars. Seat Pleasant is in Prince George's County, which everyone called "PG" for short. The PG Jaguars had a reputation for attracting some of the best talent in the area.

PG County, and all of the Washington, DC, area, had been a basketball hotbed for generations, producing great high school, college, and NBA players. When Kevin joined the Jaguars as a nine-year-old, there were two other really good players on the team—Chris Braswell and Michael Beasley. They both also lived nearby in PG County. Chris would go on to play college basketball and Michael would play in the NBA for eleven seasons.

At the time, they were like Kevin, local kids who loved playing basketball. The NBA was a far-off dream.

"My goal as a kid was to be the best player ever in my area," Kevin said. "That was my first goal even before thinking about going to college or the NBA."

Making the PG Jaguars was a step in that direction. Getting to play with his friends, compete against other good teams, and travel with Coach Craig outside of Washington, DC, to prove themselves just made it even better.

As might be expected of a US under-10 youth basketball team with two future NBA players and a Division I college star, they were good. *Really* good. A major factor in their success was the full-court press they often employed on defense. Coach Brown and Coach Craig realized Kevin and his teammates could use their size and speed to swarm their opponents in the back court and stop them from even getting the ball to half-court. Steals would lead to easy layups. The Jaguars just overwhelmed other teams. One blowout victory finished with a score of 98–7.

In the summer, Coach Craig began taking the team to tournaments up and down the East Coast. The trips were thrilling for Kevin and his friends. While they got to stay in hotels, the team was still pretty ragtag, though. Many of the teams they played were better organized and had more funding. The PG Jaguars would often play in just matching T-shirts rather than official team uniforms.

"We had no money," Coach Brown told *Deadspin*, "but we'd play all these teams in tournaments that had the nice warm-ups and the nicest jerseys . . . and we'd walk into the gym and we've got these ugly jerseys and no warm-ups . . . People laughed at us because we couldn't even dress."

They stopped laughing once the game started.

Over a three-year period, the PG Jaguars won seventeen different tournaments and compiled a record of 123–9. Years later, Kevin asked designers at Nike to make a special shoe to remember those times. It was called the KD II "PG Jaguars" and featured the team's colors—black, purple, and yellow.

On the summer nights when Kevin was home,

he, his older brother, Tony, and some of his friends would go over to a local park that was called the "King Dome." It wasn't much, just a small, simple place in the nearby city of Fairmont Heights. There were two tennis courts and a big field for baseball or football.

And, of course, there was a basketball court—one that had lighting, which meant ball could be played well into the night, sometimes even after midnight.

The King Dome would attract many of the best players in the area, even if the court was outdoors, on blacktop, and the air on so many summer nights was hot and humid. Kevin was still in middle school then, but the games featured high school kids, college kids, even grown men.

Since there was only one court and a lot of people who wanted to play, the rules were simple. These were five-on-five games and if you won, your team got to keep playing. If you lost, you had to get in the back of the line with the other waiting teams, which could mean sitting for a long time.

The games were not the most fundamentally sound or best organized, but it taught anyone who played the importance of winning. If not, your night playing ball might be over after a single loss. Since everyone wanted to keep playing, the games often got intense and physical at the end.

"Only the strongest survive out there," Kevin said. "They didn't care who you were, how old you were. If you were on the court, you were playing. And I was a skinny twelve- thirteen-year-old out there playing with grown men sometimes. And they wouldn't take it easy on me. But that built toughness. I always wanted to win. I would lose so much out there but that just molded me into who I am today."

When Kevin was ten, he and Michael Beasley went to watch a huge three-on-three tournament called "Hoop-It-Up" in Washington, DC. They were too young to play in the tournament, which featured hundreds of teams of high school kids and grown men. They just wanted to watch. But the pair of friends quickly got tired of that, so they found an empty court and started playing with teams that were waiting around for their next tournament game.

Even though their opponents were far older and stronger, Kevin began to prove he could hang with the best. He wasn't just an athletic kid. He could use his dribble to create space between himself and the defender and then pull up and shoot a long jumper. His shocking performance drew a crowd and soon people began to cheer him on. No one had ever seen a kid that young play with such skill.

"All the dudes on the mic were saying, 'Get this kid an agent,'" Beasley told *ESPN the Magazine* years later. "Everybody else [who was] out there [was] twenty-five."

"Get this kid an agent" meant they thought Kevin should sign with a sports agent and go to the NBA right then. It was a joke. No ten-year-old, no matter how good, can compete at that level. However, it was a clear sign that Kevin might have a future as a professional ballplayer. He didn't need an agent then, but he might one day.

For a lot of kids, that kind of attention would go to their head. Kevin saw it differently. He knew he had a real chance to make the NBA, but only if he did everything the right way. He didn't hear the praise and think it was a sure thing. He heard the praise and saw it as a reminder that he had talent—talent that could either be used or squandered. And anytime he missed a bunch of shots or had a bad game, he immediately began to question if he was even a good player. Kevin often focused too heavily on his mistakes.

"I lacked confidence early," Kevin told *ESPN the Magazine*. "When I didn't play well, my confidence always took a hit. So it was always up and down."

Despite the fun Kevin had at those pick-up games and tournaments, Coach Brown wasn't a fan of the King Dome or Hoop-It-Up. He felt that such games, while enjoyable, weren't serious enough. Since the style of play was often rooted in one-on-one matchups, it could lead to the development of selfish or sloppy play. Just chucking up long jumpers to get a crowd to shout was fine on a playground, but that wasn't how NBA players do it.

Instead Coach Brown wanted Kevin to concentrate on playing the game the right way, rather than adopt bad habits. After all, the goal here was to make the pros, not become a legend at the King Dome. Kevin didn't like losing out on the fun of playing at the park, but he knew Coach Brown was right. It would be the end of the King Dome for Kevin.

Kevin was self-motivated, though. That included his non-basketball life. He was always a dedicated student, in part because while he wasn't sure he could make the NBA, he recognized from a young age that he needed good grades to get a college scholarship. It also allowed him to avoid much of the trouble that other kids his age in PG County got into. He was never involved in gangs, drugs, or drinking. He was friendly with everyone in his neighborhood, but to him a fun Friday night was getting in extra shots at the activity center, not going to a party.

Kevin's biggest weakness was . . . his weakness. He was six feet tall while still in middle school, but had grown so tall, so fast, that he couldn't keep any weight on. He was incredibly skinny, no matter what he ate. His attempts to build strength through push-ups or running didn't seem to work either. Kevin was very talented on the court, but defenders could always outmuscle him and push him around. He developed a nickname—"Cookie"—because they believed he would crumble easily on contact. Kevin didn't get mad when he heard that, he just tried to use it as motivation.

Coach Brown often made him sit and write out motivational sayings as a way to pound the lesson home. One of Coach Brown's favorites became one of Kevin's favorites:

Hard work beats talent when talent fails to work hard.

Each time he scribbled that down, Kevin vowed he'd never be outworked, no matter how much talent he had. Often, soon after he was done, he and Coach Brown would head to the Hill to prove it.

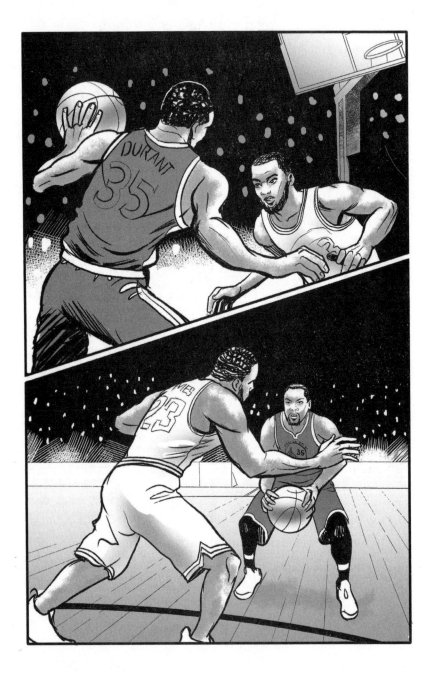

4
High School

THE SUCCESS OF THE PG Jaguars, and word of Kevin's strong play, started to spread around the area. Everyone began to realize this kid from Seat Pleasant had the potential to do big things.

That included the basketball coach at National Christian Academy, an elite college preparatory, private high school in PG County around a thirty-minute drive from Kevin's home. Kevin had always attended the local public schools and thought he would join his brother, Tony, on the team at Suitland High School.

Instead he had the opportunity to join National Christian Academy, or NCA as it was known, on a full-tuition scholarship.

NCA wasn't just known for great academics; it also had a strong basketball team that played a national schedule of top tournaments. Playing at NCA would allow Kevin to use basketball to get a great education while playing against some of the best players and teams in the country.

The only downside is that the team was loaded with good players, so Kevin wasn't just going to be handed a starting position, or even any position on the varsity at all. He was just a fourteen-year-old freshman, after all. It's one thing to dominate other players your age; it's another when you are matched up with eighteen-year-old seniors. After tryouts, Kevin was put on the junior varsity. He accepted that. It was the same old Kevin, always ready to do whatever it took to improve. He knew his time would come.

NCA was an adjustment for Kevin, and not just on the basketball court. The school was strict and the teachers were there to push students toward college. That meant challenging classes and a lot of homework. Many of the other students came from two-parent families that could afford to pay tuition to the school. NCA was not a wealthy school, but it was wealthier than what Kevin was used to.

His father, Wayne Pratt, had come back into his life at this point, trying to reestablish a relationship with Kevin and at times helping out the family financially. His involvement with Kevin was inconsistent, though. Sometimes Kevin's father would be there for him and sometimes he wouldn't. Kevin constantly struggled with the situation. He wanted his father to want to be part of his life, and it was painful and confusing when his father chose otherwise. And no matter what, money remained tight.

Kevin adjusted as he always did, by taking the higher standards at NCA as something to embrace. He figured it would all help him be a better person in the end, sort of like running the Hill or any of the other grueling drills Coach Brown put him through. And socially he had always been likable, a guy who floated between friend groups and tried to get along with everyone. He quickly felt at home.

By midseason, after an impressive showing at the junior varsity level, he had even been moved up to the varsity team, a rare accomplishment for a freshman at a powerhouse such as National Christian. He wasn't playing much, but it was clear that the coaches saw great potential in him. On many nights, Kevin was so determined to take his game to the next level that he would finish his NCA practice and then travel to the Seat Pleasant Activity Center, where either Coach Brown or Coach Craig would put him through an additional workout.

That summer, the PG Jaguars broke up. It was a great team, but it wasn't at the top level of the travel league, or AAU basketball as it is often called. Coach Brown didn't want to hold any of his talented young players back, so each one quickly joined one of the big-name teams in the area. Michael and Kevin wound up on different teams, but to this day remain friends.

Kevin's new team was called the DC Blue Devils. It was sponsored by Nike and participated in all of the big national tournaments and camps. This was just the kind of fancy, well-funded team the PG Jaguars used to enjoy defeating. Now Kevin was playing alongside not just some of the best players from his corner of PG County, but the best players from all over what locals call the DMV (DC, Maryland, Virginia). With the Jaguars, Kevin always started and rarely came out of games. Now playing on a stacked team with kids from all over the place, he had to fight to get into games.

It proved to be a big summer for Kevin because he got truly big—he grew around six inches, rising from around six foot one to six foot seven. It happened so quickly that it felt like he was adding an inch almost every night. Clothes his mom bought at the beginning of the summer no longer fit by the end of it. And the shoes that Nike provided the DC Blue Devils for him had to be turned in for larger and larger pairs.

The added height somehow made Kevin even skinnier than before. His jersey hung from his shoulders like it was on a coat hanger. His limbs sometimes moved like there weren't even any bones in them. Kevin kept eating and eating, but it didn't help. He was thin and still growing.

By the time Kevin returned for his sophomore season at NCA, it was clear he was going to be an important part of the varsity. He had managed to keep his coordination through his growth spurt, so while he wasn't very strong, he could still dribble and shoot.

NCA played an early season tournament in Delaware. It attracted a number of the top high school teams along the East Coast as well as college coaches who came to scout and recruit players that might catch their eye. Russell Springmann was one of those college coaches. He was an assistant coach at the University of Texas (UT).

While Coach Springmann worked in Texas, he grew up in Silver Spring, Maryland, not too far from Seat Pleasant. When he saw that NCA was playing, he sat down to scout them, if only out of some hometown pride. That's when he noticed this tall, incredibly thin player hit a three-point shot from the corner. Kevin was still an unknown for college scouts, but Springmann began to watch him closely. He liked Kevin's athletic ability, his jump shot, and the all-out effort he gave to the game.

"A lot of times with very talented players, they only want to be the star," Russell said. "Because Kevin was so young, and played for such a good team, he was more of a role player then. But he played very hard. That really impressed me."

Coach Springmann asked around about Kevin and learned he was just a fifteen-year-old sophomore. Boy, he thought, if this kid could gain some weight and muscle, he could be incredible. When he returned to Austin, Texas, he immediately told the Longhorns head coach, Rick Barnes, about Kevin.

Not too long after that, they extended Kevin his first college scholarship offer.

Kevin didn't immediately accept it. He was only a sophomore and had plenty of time to make his decision. He wanted to see what else was out there. The first offer made an impact on him, though, especially as he got to know Coach Springmann and Coach Barnes. He liked that Texas saw something in him before anyone else, and even though Austin was a long way from DC, he began to consider it.

"I always dreamed of playing in college and the NBA, but when Texas offered me, it felt like something that was real, that could happen for me," Kevin said. "It really helped me focus."

When NCA reeled off a 27–3 season with Kevin as a major contributor, he was inundated with scholarship offers. All of a sudden everyone saw what Coach Springmann saw. That included national powerhouses such as the University of North Carolina (UNC), Duke University, and the University of Connecticut (UConn), plus talented local universities such as Maryland and Georgetown. Unlike those schools, Texas had never won a national championship. But that didn't matter to Kevin. He was still interested in UT.

Kevin was also considering another option: entering the NBA directly out of high school. That's what future Hall of Fame players such as Kobe Bryant and Kevin Garnett had done, and it's what a high school star from Akron, Ohio, named LeBron James would do in June of 2003. At the time, the best players were skipping college altogether.

As much as getting a college education was important to Kevin, he knew earning millions of dollars in the NBA would change his and his family's life forever. His mother had worked so hard to provide him with the stability he needed, but it was always a struggle. Plus, his ultimate dream was to become a pro.

Coach Brown, Coach Craig, and others thought that Kevin was still a long way off from being able to compete at that level. First, he would need to increase his work ethic and strength—but the goal was on everyone's radar.

The question was, could Kevin rise to the occasion?

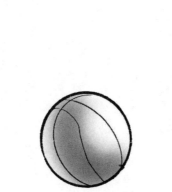

5

Oak Hill

MOUTH OF WILSON, VIRGINIA, is a small town that sits deep in the mountains in the southwest corner of the state. It is almost a six-hour drive from Washington, DC. Other than a little general store, there are almost no businesses there—certainly no malls, fast-food restaurants, or movie theaters. If you're in the mood for pizza, you have to drive almost forty-five minutes away on winding country roads to find the closest restaurant.

It is a very unlikely location for the best high school basketball team in America.

The team represents Oak Hill Academy, a small boarding school located in Mouth of Wilson. Under legendary coach Steve Smith, it's been able to attract nearly three dozen future NBA players and hundreds of college stars from all over America. They live in dormitories on campus so they can concentrate on just two things . . . school and basketball.

Oak Hill's teams are so good that they play a true national schedule, challenging the best teams from across the country and competing in the very best tournaments. The team's games usually air on ESPN a couple of times a year and Oak Hill has been named national champions ten times by *USA Today*.

Players find that a year or two at Oak Hill allows them to get away from all the distractions of home. With nothing much to do but study and play, they can concentrate on improving their game. Coach Smith spends a great deal of time on individual development and teaching students how the game should be played through long, tough practices. And during those practices, not to mention pick-up games with teammates, some of the best players in the country match up against each other. If you can withstand the pressure, you're bound to improve.

Since Kevin was always looking to get better,

when Oak Hill came calling, he accepted the pressure. If joining this elite team was what it would take to get the attention of scouts from the NBA, not just the National Collegiate Athletic Association (NCAA), then he would kiss his mother goodbye and move to Mouth of Wilson. The city kid was willing to go country for a while.

"It's in the middle of nowhere, first off," Kevin told ESPN. "It's right dead-center in a bunch of woods. But it was great exposure. We played on ESPN three times, went to the biggest tournaments in the country, had the best coaches, and got to play with the best players. It's good for your game."

The move wasn't easy. "It was far away from home," Kevin said. "It was tough being away from my family." Still, he fit in fine. One of his teammates from the DC Blue Devils, Ty Lawson, moved there as well. They all agreed the total-basketball environment helped them improve. At night, when practice and homework were done, the guys would normally return to the gym to put in more work or play among themselves.

"All you can do is play basketball and go to school," Kevin told ESPN.

Actually, in the spring, after the basketball season

was over, but before school was done, Kevin was so bored he decided to play baseball. He was a first baseman, but he said he lasted just three games because he kept striking out. It was clear basketball was his sport.

The team would finish 34–2 and win another national title. Kevin slowly improved his outside shot and became known as one of the best players in America. In one of Oak Hill's rare close games, they entered the fourth quarter trailing by nine points. Kevin, who had learned to thrive under pressure, erased that deficit by hitting four three-pointers. Oak Hill won by three. Kevin averaged 19.6 points and 8.8 rebounds a game and was considered one of the top five players nationally in the Class of 2006 on all the recruiting lists.

Coach Smith thought Kevin would be back for his senior season, especially when word broke that Kevin's old friend Michael Beasley was enrolling at Oak Hill, too.

Instead, Kevin decided he wanted to return to Washington, DC, for his final year of high school. He figured he was already going to move away after graduation, either to go to college or the NBA. That meant this would be his final chance to live with his mom and be around his grandmother and father, who was also now fully active in his life.

Wayne Pratt regretted the time he'd spent away from his family, and while he and Kevin's mother would never get back together, he began doing anything he could to be involved with his sons. He worked as a Capitol police officer at the Library of Congress in Washington, DC, but if after work he needed to drive all the way to Mouth of Wilson to watch one of Kevin's games, and then back to DC when it was done, then he'd do it.

"I just gave them everything I had," Wayne Pratt told *The Washington Post*. "I emptied the tank. There wasn't a place I wouldn't go; there wasn't nothing I wouldn't do . . . It's never too late to be your kid's father. It's never too late. You have to try. We all make mistakes."

It was better late than never. Kevin appreciated his father's efforts, and the fact that he knew even if he did make it to the NBA, his dad vowed to continue to work as a police officer. Wayne didn't want his son thinking he was only back in his life because he was a star athlete who was about to make millions in the NBA. Finally, Wayne believed he was ready to be a father.

"He always wants to support me," Kevin said.

Of course, Kevin's mother never had the luxury of making such a choice, which his dad understood. As a result, he was both apologetic and thankful. He understood that too many kids are left to grow up in single-family households, especially in the African American community. He was also appreciative of Coach Brown, who served as a father figure to his son when he was growing up.

"He was there when I wasn't there," Wayne Pratt told *The Washington Post*. "And I continually thank him for that, because he didn't have to do that . . . I thought that was very noble of him."

There were other reasons Kevin wanted to move back home. One was a trainer he met by the name of Alan Stein, who worked with the basketball program at Montrose Christian School in Rockville, Maryland. The high school was coached by Stu Vetter, who through the years had built a very successful club that had produced dozens of top players. It wasn't Oak Hill, but it was close.

Despite Vetter's reputation, it was Stein, who interested Kevin most. His year at Oak Hill had increased his status with scouts and proven to everyone he was among the very best, if not the best, player in his class. He was still skinny for his height, just 185 or so pounds, and couldn't figure out how to gain weight or strength, which would hurt him with NBA teams. Stein said he could help and dared Kevin to work out with him just once. Afterward, Kevin was exhausted but convinced this intense training regimen was what he needed.

As always, Kevin did everything with purpose. He enrolled at Montrose Christian, even though his commute from Seat Pleasant required catching two trains and took over an hour each way.

The final reason Kevin came home was because tragedy had struck. In late April of the year Kevin was at Oak Hill, his old AAU coach, Chuckie Craig, had gone out with some friends to a bar in PG County. At the end of the night, there was a fight between two groups of men outside in the parking lot. It was pouring rain and there was a lot of confusion. As Coach Craig walked back to his car, a man came up behind him with a gun and fired. Coach Craig fell to the ground and was soon pronounced dead.

The news shocked Kevin. Coach Craig was someone he had spent endless hours with, not just working on small parts of his game but laughing, joking, and talking about life. Now, suddenly, he was gone. As a tribute, Kevin later switched his uniform number, which was usually 32, to 35, because Coach Craig was thirty-five years old when he died. He wanted Coach Craig to be a part of his basketball journey, which he'd helped inspire. Kevin's jersey, of course, would become one of the top-selling jerseys in the NBA, worn by fans all around the world.

"Without them knowing, they've got a piece of Chuck on," Kevin told *The Oklahoman*. "I just want as many people as I can to know why I wear it and the significance of the number. That's my goal, to get him out there and keep his name alive."

Back home for his senior year, Kevin excelled on the court for Montrose Christian. He averaged 23.6 points, 10.2 rebounds, 3.0 assists, 3.0 steals, and 2.6 blocks per game while leading Montrose Christian to a 20–2 record. They finished ranked ninth in the final *USA Today* poll. His workouts with Alan Stein helped build some strength, although he still struggled to gain weight. He was naturally thin. Changing that would take years, and even today, he's not a particularly muscular guy as far as NBA players are concerned.

The most memorable game came when they took on none other than Oak Hill Academy late in the season. Oak Hill was ranked number one in the nation and had won fifty-four consecutive games, dating back to Kevin's time on the team. Before an overflowing crowd of four thousand at a high school gym in Washington, DC, Kevin led Montrose to a 74–72 victory, scoring thirty-one points in a come-from-behind win over his old school. Oak Hill would finish 40–1.

The game was shown on local cable television and would cement Kevin as one of the greatest high school players to ever come out of the DMV.

Kevin wasn't just considered great for his area, though. He was rated as the number two recruit in America behind a seven-foot center from Indianapolis named Greg Oden. Kevin was named a first team All-American by *USA Today*, was a co-MVP of the McDonald's All American game, which plays host to some of the best high school stars in the country, and represented the United States in the Nike Hoop Summit.

By this point Kevin stood at least six foot nine and wore a size eighteen shoe, though he played even bigger.

Even with his slight frame, Kevin was a talent that NBA teams wanted. Yet he no longer had the option to jump directly from high school to the NBA. The league had instituted a minimum age requirement, the so-called "one-and-done" rule. Now a player had to be at least one year removed from high school to be drafted. That meant Kevin needed to spend at least one year playing college basketball.

Just about every school in the country wanted him on their team. He was leaning toward the University of North Carolina, which always had a strong team and was where NBA legend Michael Jordan had played. Yet Coach Springmann and Coach Barnes had never stopped pushing him to consider playing for the University of Texas. That long show of loyalty mattered to Kevin.

There were plenty of good reasons to go to UT. It had a great strength and conditioning coach who Kevin felt could help him continue his efforts to add muscle and weight. It had a number of starters who were about to graduate, meaning Kevin could get plenty of playing time right away, showcasing his game to potential NBA suitors. Texas was also a great academic school and Austin was a fun city to live in, even if it was far from PG County.

"We said, 'hey, we've lost our entire team. We've got four guys coming back. If we want to really be a special team, you're going to have to come in and want to have a Player of the Year–type year. You'll have to put that together for us,'" Coach Barnes said.

"We actually said to him, 'you're going to have the chance to do it because you're going to get the minutes,'" Coach Barnes continued.

The chance to step in and be the focal point of a college team and try to become the National Player of the Year while improving his game for the NBA was too much to pass up. No, Texas wasn't a traditional powerhouse such as UNC or Duke, but Kevin said he "wanted to blaze [his] own trail."

And with that, Kevin Durant was headed to Texas.

6

Texas

WHEN KEVIN ARRIVED at the University of Texas, everyone assumed he'd only stay one year and then immediately declare for the NBA draft. This was the first year of the "one-and-done" rule. While college basketball fans and coaches were excited to watch players of Kevin's caliber, there were questions about just how dedicated they would be if they were only going to college because the rules said they must.

Kevin didn't want anyone to think he was that type of person. He wasn't in Austin just to pass the time. He was there to become a better player, but also to be a regular college student, be a great teammate, and help the Longhorns win games.

And he immediately proved himself to be a team player. When Kevin and teammate A. J. Abrams were slated to attend a preseason media day for the Big 12 Conference, which Texas plays in, Kevin told Coach Barnes he didn't want to go unless all his teammates were allowed to come and receive attention. That wasn't how it worked, so Kevin and A.J. attended, but the point was made.

During the season, Kevin appeared on the cover of *Sports Illustrated*. It was a prestigious honor, except he didn't like all the attention focused on him. "I never like to be singled out," he said. "I'm with fourteen [teammates]. And I try and shy away from this . . . It's great, but I came here to win games. That's what I'm trying to do for my team . . . those accolades [are] always good, but I want to win."

Winning in college wouldn't be simple. Kevin had always worked hard to improve his game, but he'd also almost always either been the best player on the court or been surrounded by so many other great players that he was on the best team. Victories had come easy. So had open looks. Throughout his final three years in high school, at National Christian, Oak Hill, and Montrose Christian, he'd lost just seven games.

College basketball was different. Every team had great players, many of them four years older and much bigger and stronger than Kevin. Plus, every team had great coaching, meaning Kevin would be dealing with defensive game plans designed to make the game difficult for him. Conversely, he was expected to play defense with the same energy level he expended on offense—something that only occasionally had been needed in high school, where blocking the shots of shorter players was somewhat easy.

Coach Rick Barnes is known for his sense of humor, and while recruiting Kevin, he showed it. Once Kevin was on campus, though, Coach Barnes's demanding side came out. Practices were harder than any Kevin had ever dealt with. He also had more responsibilities on the court. And no mistake occurred without Coach Barnes letting him know about it.

"I told him before the season started, 'you know, you've got a chance to be National Player of the Year,'" Coach Barnes said. "Obviously I had a selfish motive in that because if he is the National Player of the Year, we're going to be pretty good. [I said,] 'but to do that you have to improve defensively, you're going to have to rebound the ball, you can't just sit out there and shoot threes.'"

Kevin loved the challenge. He loved how important all of the practices and games were. He loved the support staff. The Texas training staff realized that Kevin rarely ate breakfast in high school. He was usually running late and only occasionally would chomp down on a candy bar. They forced him to improve his nutrition and he quickly gained ten pounds, moving up to 215 on the scale. That was a good step, but then preseason conditioning was so rigorous, Kevin lost weight.

Watching Kevin work just as hard, if not harder, than anyone on the team inspired confidence in him from his teammates and coaches. It means something to the rest of the team when their best player is also the most dedicated. Kevin strived to be that type of leader. He was constantly seeking the coaches' opinions about his defensive play. He'd stay after practice not only to put up extra shots, but also to watch the coaches' film of the practice to see how he could improve.

"We knew he was a great talent," Coach Barnes

said. "The thing that makes him what he is, is he's so unselfish. He doesn't have an ego . . . I think from the time he walked on this campus, people loved him because he didn't want to be treated any differently. He wants to be coached like anybody else. The guys love him for that. I think with all the attention that he's gotten, he's really—it hasn't changed him one bit. And that's probably what makes him really special."

Fans and media didn't know what to make of the Longhorns coming into the season. They had lost four starters and were reliant on freshmen, but one of them was Kevin Durant. In the preseason poll of the best teams in the country, they checked in at number twenty-one. At the start of the season, they played like a typical new group trying to find their rhythm. They won two, then lost one. They won three, then lost one. They won three more, then lost again.

Kevin's play was also uneven. He scored twenty-one points and grabbed nine rebounds against Michigan State University, which were decent stats. However, he shot just one of eight from three-point range and scored just five points in the second half as State won. In the next game, Kevin had twenty-nine points and ten rebounds in a victory over St. John's University. Best of all, he hit five of six three-pointers.

Basketball fans around the country started to take notice, but Coach Barnes thought Kevin hadn't even come close to reaching his full potential since he was improving by the day.

"Kevin hasn't played well yet," Coach Barnes said.

Yet?

"He is progressing well," Coach Barnes said. "He is two hundred miles from where he was two weeks ago. He's special."

A stat line of twenty-nine points and ten rebounds is an impressive performance, so naturally people wondered: How much better could he really get?

Kevin was about to show them. He was about to take over the college basketball season.

He poured in thirty-seven points and sixteen rebounds against the University of Colorado. Then thirty-four and thirteen against the University of Missouri, followed by thirty-seven points, twelve rebounds, and four blocks in a loss at Oklahoma State University.

"He's an unreal talent," Oklahoma State coach Sean Sutton marveled.

Kevin became a phenomenon. Texas games on television began drawing huge ratings as fans, both of college and the NBA, wanted to see what Kevin would do next. Meanwhile, attendance at home games grew, with around thirteen thousand fans coming out for each game. It was no different during road games in the Big 12 Conference, where the Longhorns arrived like rock stars.

Kevin's combination of size and skills was almost unheard of and he just kept delivering. His teammates even began calling him "Showtime."

There were thirty-four points and nine rebounds against Baylor University. Then came an astounding thirty-seven points and twenty-three rebounds at Texas Tech University, which left even Tech's Hall of Fame coach, Bob Knight, one of the all-time greats, in awe.

"He's really good," Coach Knight said. "The guy is six-nine. He's mobile, he's quick, he's fast. What more does he have to do? There's no secret. There is no secret thing that he drinks before the game that makes him good . . . The guy is a great athlete that can really play basketball."

Kevin was unstoppable in that game against Texas Tech, hitting fifteen of twenty-nine shots. But what really impressed the UT coaches was what he said to them in the locker room after the game.

"The first thing he said to me was, 'Coach, how was my defense tonight?'" Coach Springmann said.

Even after such an outstanding performance, he was focused on the ways he could improve.

On and on it went—thirty-two points, thirty points, thirty-two more. Teams tried to double-team him, employ a zone defense, and use all sorts of tricks. Nothing seemed to slow him down.

The occasional games when Kevin didn't score at least thirty, fans were almost disappointed. Kevin put up twenty-one points and snared twelve rebounds in an 83–54 blowout victory of Oklahoma State University, but he noticed that the Texas fans didn't even cheer that loudly when he came out of the game.

"I hope they weren't disappointed," Kevin said. "I had a double-double and we won. But I know what you mean . . ."

"I mean, look at his night," Coach Barnes said with a laugh. "That's a great night for anybody. People would like that. But expectations . . ."

Kevin was well on his way to becoming the consensus National Player of the Year, beating out Greg Oden, the seven-foot center who attended Ohio State University and had been rated above him coming out of high school.

Yet no matter how big the hoopla got, Kevin kept trying to remain a typical college kid. He kept up with his schoolwork, even as everyone asked him why he was bothering since he was about to become a multimillionaire in the NBA. But to Kevin, the education was an opportunity and he didn't want to squander it.

When he wasn't studying or working on his game, Kevin walked around the campus, hung out with friends, and even volunteered to be a scorekeeper for the school's intramural basketball league. When word got out, fans started coming to those games to get his autograph, which meant there were suddenly a lot of people watching intramurals. Kevin loved it. He loved it all. He may have been a star player, but he felt like a normal college student.

"The guys on my team keep me level-headed because they're always joking around and things like that," Kevin said. "It's all fun. I love being at Texas. This is the best place."

The question basketball-wise was how far Kevin

could lead Texas in the postseason—first the Big 12 Tournament, then the NCAAs, also known as March Madness.

The team was still young and inconsistent. The Longhorns weren't title favorites. But they had Kevin and a lot of chemistry. "We are not a one-man team," Kevin kept reminding everyone.

The Big 12 Conference held its championship tournament in Oklahoma City and fans packed the arena to see if Kevin would put on a show. He didn't disappoint, scoring a record ninety-two points in three games. That included twenty-four in the second half to lead a comeback against Baylor and finally an amazing thirty-seven points, ten rebounds, six blocks, and two steals in a title game loss to favored University of Kansas.

"I don't want to play him again," Kansas coach Bill Self said with a laugh. "I mean, this guy is a joke. He is a joke. You can plug him into any team in the country at any level and he can score. NBA, whatever, just plug him in and he can go get baskets. It's unbelievable how good he is."

Up next, the NCAA Tournament. This, Kevin knew, was when all of America, not just avid college basketball fans, tuned in. Kevin and his teammates wanted to prove to everyone that Texas could hang with the best and reach the Final Four.

They came out nervous in their first game, however. Despite being heavy favorites, they needed a late rally to beat an underdog New Mexico State University team. Kevin had twenty-seven points and eight rebounds while facing double and triple teams. Still, Coach Barnes was concerned the team wasn't assertive enough.

In the second round, Texas faced a much bigger challenge, a deep, athletic University of Southern California team that was coached by Tim Floyd, who used to coach in the NBA. Coach Barnes designed a game plan that would let Kevin shoot, figuring he was going to score a lot of points no matter what. However, USC wanted to make it as difficult as possible, all while shutting down the other Longhorns, most notably guard D. J. Augustin.

The USC game plan was perfect. Kevin scored thirty, but he needed twenty-four shots to get there. Meanwhile Augustin went one for eight and Texas fell behind early and never truly challenged USC. USC had five different players score in double figures and won easily 87–68. Coach Floyd took time after the game, however, to talk about how impressed he was with Kevin and how, based on his time in the NBA, he thought Kevin was going to make a big impact.

"The thing that impresses me about him is his approach to how he's gotten to this level of greatness," Coach Floyd said. "I wish that more players in our country understood that this kid wasn't out playing street ball, and wasn't playing pick-up games, that he was locked in a gym in DC for seven years working on individual skills. He's not great because he's six-ten. He's great because he knows how to play the game and he has a skill package that allows him to play."

Kevin said the loss left a "sour taste" in his mouth. He wanted Texas to go further in the NCAA Tournament. With the season over, though, he had a big, if obvious, decision to make. Come back for another year or enter the NBA draft? After talking it over with his family, he did what most expected.

"It's a dream come true," Kevin said.

He was one and done at college. The NBA was calling.

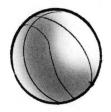

7

The NBA

THE PORTLAND TRAIL BLAZERS had the first
pick in the 2007 NBA draft, which meant General
Manager Kevin Pritchard didn't just have a big decision to make, he also received a lot of unsolicited
advice about whom he should take.

There were two obvious choices for the top spot
in the draft—Kevin and Ohio State freshman Greg
Oden. Kevin had put up dazzling stats and highlight
reel plays while being named National Player of the
Year. Greg, though, was a dominating seven-foot,
250-pound center who led his team to the NCAA

Championship Game before falling just short of a national title.

Basketball fans everywhere were torn over who would become a better pro. Kevin was a special player, but there was a belief in basketball at the time that a team needed a true center to be a championship-caliber team. After all, Ohio State had reached the NCAA Tournament title game while Texas had lost in the second round. Oden was seen as the next great classic big man, the next Tim Duncan (who won five NBA championships) or Shaquille O'Neal (winner of four NBA championships). Meanwhile, no one was certain about which position Kevin would even play.

"He has a position," Coach Barnes said. "And it's all five."

The debate—Oden or Durant—raged everywhere, not just on television and the radio, but between friends, in work break rooms, and on school playgrounds. Fans wrote letters to the Trail Blazers, making a case for one player or the other. Some hung signs in apartment windows in downtown Portland, signaling their allegiance to either Kevin or Greg. The Blazers website took polls. Everyone had an opinion.

One time Kevin Pritchard pulled his car up to a stoplight. The driver in the car next to him recognized him and immediately stood up, poked his head through the sunroof, and began shouting at Pritchard.

"Take Durant!" the man screamed. "Take Durant!"

"Let the debate begin," Pritchard said with a laugh. "Well, I guess it started a long time ago. It's funny because everybody has a very strong opinion. There is no gray area here. People either are very strong with Durant or very strong with Oden."

Kevin, for his part, said he didn't care. He didn't feel it was right to get into a debate about who was better. If he wasn't picked first by Portland, he would almost certainly get picked second overall by the Seattle SuperSonics, a team that would eventually move, change names, and become the Oklahoma City Thunder. He just wanted to get to the NBA, whether it was with the first, second, or last pick in the draft.

Besides, he liked Greg personally and didn't want it to become a rivalry that would hurt their friendship. As always, he was thinking of others.

"It doesn't really matter where I am drafted,"

Kevin said. "I just want to be there and make an impact. I'll leave that up to the people that handle the draft process. I know that I will be one of the high picks, but it doesn't matter where I go."

Kevin worked out for Portland. So did Greg. Meanwhile Kevin Pritchard and the rest of the Blazers coaches and scouts tried to make a decision. Kevin had better basic stats, 25.8 points and 11.1 rebounds a game to Greg's 15.7 points and 9.7 rebounds. However, Greg had played on a more well-rounded team and contributed an important 3.3 blocks a game.

One question that came up was about Kevin's strength. Word spread that he couldn't bench-press 185 pounds even a single time. It was a feat nearly any NBA player could accomplish. Would these grown men in the NBA just break him apart?

"If people question his strength, they're stupid," Coach Barnes said at the time, defending Kevin. "If they are looking for weightlifters to come out of Texas, that's not what we're producing. There are a lot of guys who can bench-press three hundred pounds in the NBA who couldn't play dead in a cowboy movie. Kevin's the best player in the draft, period, at any position."

Greg and Kevin had been ranked first and second coming out of high school and now they were first and second coming out of college. The only question was in which order would they go in the draft?

That was determined when the NBA commissioner at the time, David Stern, stepped up to the microphone and made the announcement as Kevin, his mom, dad, grandmother, brother, and Coach Taras Brown sat at a table in the draft's "greenroom" watching. Kevin wore a new gray suit and a burnt orange tie (the Texas Longhorns' team color) and listened closely.

"With the first pick in the 2007 NBA draft, the Portland Trail Blazers select Greg Oden from Ohio State University," Commissioner Stern announced.

Greg jumped up from his seat and began hugging his family. Kevin smiled and clapped. He was truly fine with the outcome.

"I didn't know who he was going to pick," Kevin said. "I held my mother's hand and we both looked at each other in the eye and when he said 'Greg,' I figured where I was going to be going next. I'm happy for Greg. I went and gave his mom a hug and a kiss and congratulated their family."

Moments later, Commissioner Stern announced Seattle had picked Kevin, and with that came the family celebration, embraces, and even some tears of joy. It had been a long road to this point, so much work, so many twists and turns and moves. Now, at last, the moment had arrived.

"Once they called my name, I shed a few tears, and my mom shed some tears, and my brother was happy for me," Kevin said.

After being selected, Kevin sat down with ESPN and the first question from host Stuart Scott was this: "Kevin Durant's favorite quote is 'hard work beats talent when talent fails to work hard.' What does that quote mean to you, Kevin?" Kevin smiled slightly as Coach Taras Brown's old words were repeated to him. The saying had been his mantra that got him here, after all.

"It means no matter how good you are, if you don't work hard, nothing will happen for you," Kevin said. "I always use that quote. I instilled it in myself. No matter how good I am, I've got to keep working."

The real work was about to begin, in part because Kevin's rookie season would not go as smoothly as he'd envisioned.

Some of it was a dream come true. He moved into a spacious home and his mom came along to cook for him and take care of running the house. He signed endorsement deals with Nike and Gatorade. EA Sports put him on the cover of its *NCAA March Madness 08* video game. "I'm going to be first in line to buy all the copies to hand out to all my friends," Kevin said of a game he grew up playing for fun.

Kevin had never been particularly motivated by money, but he was now incredibly wealthy. He was being paid around $4.1 million by the SuperSonics and his endorsement deals were valued at over $80 million. The Nike contract included the development of a signature shoe line.

For a kid who had once thought his family getting their own small apartment in Seat Pleasant was the greatest day of his life, the idea of never again having to worry (or have anyone in his family worry) about money was difficult to fathom. He appreciated, though, that his father stayed in Washington and continued to work his job as a Capitol police officer, enjoying his son's success but not trying to live off it.

Kevin may have been a very wealthy NBA player,

but he was still just a teenager. His teammates were older, some of them in their thirties, with wives and children of their own. He didn't always have a lot in common with them. For fun, he began to invite kids in his neighborhood over to his house to hang out, watch movies, or play video games.

Kevin even became famous for wearing a backpack when he walked into the arena for games. It made him look like a college student, which he still would've been had such incredible opportunities not come calling. "I see a lot of people on Twitter hitting me, 'what's in the book bag, what's in the book bag?'" Kevin said a few years later. "It's nothing special. It's just an iPad and the Bible."

The downside to the season was that the team he joined was unstable. Seattle's home arena was considered old by NBA standards. A new ownership group, led by a businessman from Oklahoma named Clay Bennett, was demanding the city build them a new facility or they would move the team to a new town. The city government wasn't budging, though. So just as the season started, Clay Bennett announced that he was going to take the team to Oklahoma City for the 2008–09 season.

Fans were understandably upset and stopped supporting the Sonics. The atmosphere surrounding the team felt negative. The Sonics lost their first eight games of the season and later amassed a fourteen-game losing streak, which for Kevin, who was accustomed to almost always winning, felt like a shock. The Sonics finished with the worst record in the NBA at a meager 20–62.

However, on an individual level, Kevin was incredible. He averaged 20.3 points a game and netted more than thirty total on seven different occasions. In the final game of the season, he scored forty-two points and grabbed thirteen rebounds as the Sonics beat Golden State. It was like he was back in college again.

All that talk about him being too weak to make it in the NBA, or that not being able to bench-press 185 would matter, was washed away. "If a guy can play basketball, a guy can play basketball," Kevin said. For a young player on a team with little help, it was an impressive season. He was named the NBA Rookie of the Year.

Greg Oden, meanwhile, played just sixty-one (out of eighty-two) games and struggled with injuries, which would soon end his career. Greg played parts of just three seasons in the NBA and never panned out due to health issues.

Kevin didn't take satisfaction in proving he

should have been the top pick. Instead he felt bad for Greg, who remains a very likable guy and was a great player.

"He didn't want to get hurt," Kevin said, defending his friend years later from fan criticism. "That was the last thing he wanted to do . . . But when he did play, he was a force."

● ● ●

There was one benefit to finishing in last place for the now Oklahoma City Thunder: They were able to draft some talent to help Kevin. They chose a guard from the University of California, Los Angeles (UCLA) named Russell Westbrook and a six-ten big man from the Republic of Congo in Africa named Serge Ibaka. Combined with another young player, forward Jeff Green, the Thunder may not have been very experienced, but they did have some long-term potential in their new city.

That played out across the season as the team, particularly Kevin and Russell, learned to play together. It was ugly early on—the Thunder started 3–29 on the year and looked like they might be one of the worst teams in NBA history.

Yet by midseason, under new coach Scott Brooks, things began to change. OKC went 20–30 to close the year and while their overall record (23–59) was still bad, there was optimism. Kevin believed the team could actually make the playoffs in 2009–10.

One thing Kevin discovered upon moving to Oklahoma City was a community-wide passion for the team that hadn't been possible in Seattle because fans were angry that the franchise was about to abandon them.

In OKC, everything the Thunder did was exciting. Oklahoma had never had a permanent pro team in any sport. The local fans generally watched college sports—the University of Oklahoma or Oklahoma State University—or rooted for a pro team from a different state, usually the ones in Dallas, Texas. Now they had a team to call their own.

Fans packed the Ford Center downtown, adorned their cars with Thunder bumper stickers, and watched nearly every game, even with all the losses.

The Thunder were just getting settled into town. That first year, they practiced in a converted roller-skating rink that sat near a dog food plant, causing unsavory smells to sometimes waft in. Kevin, Russ, and the others didn't care. They were young guys looking to build something, so they spent nearly every waking hour at the facility.

For the 2009–10 season, the Thunder added

another great young player, scoring guard James Harden, who was drafted third overall from Arizona State University. As the Thunder continued to gel and gain experience, it was clear that General Manager Sam Presti had done an amazing job building a young nucleus through the draft.

Kevin would average 30.1 points a game that year to edge out LeBron James (29.7) and lead the NBA in scoring. Russell followed with 16.1 points and Harden, who wasn't even a starter, averaged 9.9 points. All of them were twenty-one years old or younger at the time.

By midseason, Kevin's optimism about a playoff appearance looked realistic. The team was athletic, fast, and exciting, often draining long threes or slamming home dunks.

Late in the season, OKC traveled to Boston to play the Celtics, who were the defending NBA champions. It was just a regular season game, but the Thunder felt like it was a chance to make a statement that they weren't just a bunch of young kids. That day Kevin scored thirty-seven, Russ added twenty-one, and the Thunder won in Boston.

"We've grown up," Kevin told reporters after the game.

Indeed, they had. Kevin was named to the All-Star game for the first time, another milestone, although he was the proudest of having the team reach the fifty-win plateau (50–32) and qualify, as he'd predicted, for the playoffs.

The Thunder had come a long way, but their road was about to end. They were defeated 4–2 in the opening round by a Kobe Bryant–led Los Angeles Lakers team that would win the NBA championship that year. Kevin averaged 25.0 points and 7.7 rebounds a game in that series. He made a statement by often playing as well as Kobe, who was one of the NBA's all-time great players. It wasn't enough, so the loss to the Lakers was a disappointment. There was no doubt, however, that this franchise was headed upward.

And quickly.

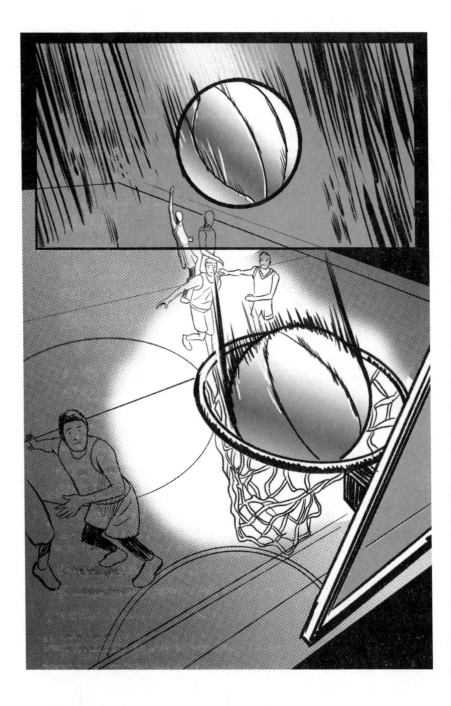

8

Thunder

KEVIN DURANT. Russell Westbrook. James Harden.

Soon enough, each player would be a perennial NBA All-Star, a household name, and a regular in commercials for everything from shoes to sodas.

In the fall of 2010 though, they were still a bit of a mystery to the NBA. Oklahoma City was this new team, in this small market, and here were these three young guns making noise. Everyone could see they had talent, but could a group so new and inexperienced really compete for a championship? Usually teams needed to build up slowly with a mix of veterans and big-name stars. OKC was just bursting onto the scene.

Kevin believed they could do it because he saw what was happening every day in practice—first at that old roller rink and then at a plush new facility. As always, he was obsessed with getting better. So was Russ. And so, too, was James. The whole team was like that, really—a core that also included Serge Ibaka and Jeff Green. He'd found his equals in Coach Brown's old saying: "Hard work beats talent when talent fails to work hard."

It was a big group of players in their early twenties, mostly without family responsibilities in a city that they all enjoyed living in, but one that wasn't filled with nightlife. Only around 580,000 people lived in OKC itself at the time. That is small by NBA standards. The town is known for business and being the seat of the state government, not entertainment. There are a lot of ranches and oil wells surrounding OKC. There aren't any beaches or nightclubs to distract.

That was just fine with Kevin and the others. With little else to do, they did what they liked most . . . not just play basketball but practice basketball.

And not just practice but practice even after practice. This was often accomplished through full-throttle pick-up games that would run late into the night. When they weren't at the gym, they were at someone's house playing video games. They figured that at their age, they could all still be in college, so what was wrong with still acting like college kids? Together, they didn't just slowly develop skill and toughness on the court, but trust and friendship off of it.

"It was really AAU basketball," Kevin told the San Jose *Mercury News*. "We were just having fun. We weren't listening to anyone on the outside, media, none of that. It was just pure fun."

Kevin was ready to enter the next phase of his career. He signed a new contract, a five-year, $89 million extension with the Thunder—the kind of money and commitment that indicated he was a franchise player. There had been plenty of speculation in the media that Durant might bolt OKC for a bigger city, perhaps even for his hometown Washington Wizards. Instead he made it clear he was all in on the Thunder.

After having moved around so much due to basketball, staying in one place and putting down some roots made sense. After all, he'd played in a new city every year from the time he was a sophomore in high school through his third season in the NBA (National Christian, Oak Hill, Montrose Christian, Texas, Seattle, OKC). He was ready to build something.

Kevin also had spent the summer of 2010 helping the USA Basketball team win the World Championship. It wasn't just the extra games against physically challenging international competition that helped; it was also his time with legendary Duke coach Mike Krzyzewski, who was a master motivator to young players. Kevin spent considerable time as well with veteran guard Chauncey Billups, who had won an NBA title in Detroit and was known as one of the great leaders in the league.

It was no longer just Kevin who thought the Thunder were on the verge of something big. Everyone was watching now. They were the hot new team in the league.

For its NBA preseason issue, *Sports Illustrated* wanted to put Kevin on its cover under the title "THUNDER BALL." It was a big deal, not just for Kevin but the entire OKC franchise, which wasn't used to that kind of national publicity. Yet Kevin, just like he'd been back at Texas, was hesitant about all the focus being on him. He told *SI* that he would only appear if the picture included the entire Thunder starting five.

The magazine didn't want that many players on the cover. Having one player as the focus helped newsstand sales. They agreed to picture the other stars on a couple page spreads inside the magazine. Kevin kept pushing until *Sports Illustrated* wound up putting a picture of Kevin front and center with far lesser known teammates Nenad Krstić and Thabo Sefolosha behind him. Neither player was even a double-digit scorer for the team and would never otherwise merit a valued *SI* cover spot. Kevin, however, believed they were very important.

"Thabo and Nenad, people don't really get to talk about them too much for some odd reason, so it was good to have them on there with me," Durant told reporters at the time. "They're guys we have to have on this team, so I wanted everybody to know how important they are to us and how great teammates they are. I was happy to have a chance to voice my opinion and I'm glad *Sports Illustrated* put them on the cover with me."

To say this was an unusual move by a star player

is an understatement. Most people, understandably, seek the kind of spotlight that a magazine cover brings. It's not like Kevin didn't deserve it, and as a young player trying to build up his brand for his Nike and Gatorade endorsement deals, it was just good business.

But Kevin always put the team first. Always. And that meant a ton to everyone in the Thunder locker room.

In the middle of the season, though, the team changed. OKC was rolling along and had become a contender because of its success drafting great young players. The problem was they had too many of them, and as their rookie deals expired, each one was due a considerable raise for their next contract. The NBA has what's called a salary cap, which limits how much each team can collectively pay its players. There is only so much money in the pool. Simply put, there was no way over the next couple of years the Thunder could afford to keep Kevin, Russ, James, Serge, and Jeff. If they couldn't re-sign them, then the team risked losing the players to free agency and not getting any players back in return.

As a result, OKC traded Jeff and Nenad to the Boston Celtics in exchange for Kendrick Perkins, a big, tough forward who could help them defend and rebound. Jeff and Nenad were scorers and shooters, but the Thunder had enough scorers and shooters. They were so loaded James Harden wasn't even a starter.

Getting Perkins didn't just make OKC a better team, but one ready for the grind and intensity of the playoffs. In losing to LA the year prior, they'd showed they just weren't ready to compete at that ultimate level. Adding Perkins, a veteran who had won an NBA title in Boston, was an important step in helping solve that problem.

OKC won fifty-five games and entered the post-season as the number four seed. Kevin once again led the league in scoring, posting a 27.7 average. He was focused on winning a championship, though, and showed it in the opening game of the opening round series against Denver. A year prior, Kevin had been shut down in Game 1 against the Lakers—he needed a whopping twenty-four shot attempts to score just twenty-four points. It set the tone for the series.

This time, he made a different opening statement, scoring forty-one to lead the Thunder to a victory. OKC closed out Denver in five games, losing just one, with Kevin averaging an astounding 32.4 points in the series, including pumping in sixteen points in the fourth quarter of Game 5 to ice the series.

Next up, a tough Memphis Grizzlies team that jumped to a 2–1 series lead. But with an amazing thirty-nine-point effort from Kevin in the decisive Game 7, OKC rallied to win the series. A franchise that had never won a playoff series and just two years prior won a meager twenty-three games, was now in the Western Conference Finals against the Dallas Mavericks and their star player, Dirk Nowitzki.

Kevin, Russell, and the others were eyeing the NBA Finals, especially since it appeared the Miami Heat would come out of the East. The Heat had formed a so-called "Super Team" that offseason, when LeBron James, the best player in the NBA at the time, and big man Chris Bosh became free agents and joined Dwyane Wade in Miami. The Heat, led by "the Big Three," were heavy favorites to win the title and for Kevin, a chance to measure the Thunder against them—not to mention measure himself against LeBron—was tantalizing.

Instead, Nowitzki taught the young Thunder that each round of the playoffs becomes tougher and tougher. In Game 1, Nowitzki scored forty-eight points. Kevin had forty of his own, but Russell shot three of fifteen and the Mavs bench scored fifty-three points to help Dallas win by nine. To win games in the conference finals and beyond, you need an entire team, not just one star. Dallas kept reminding OKC of that as they cruised to a 4–1 series victory. Kevin scored a lot—28.0 points a game, but he shot under 50 percent.

A showdown with LeBron and the Heat would have to wait. There was no shame in losing to Dallas—the Mavs would go on to upset the Heat and win the title—but it was clear the Thunder just weren't ready yet to be crowned champions.

Kevin said it was a "fun" playoff run, but it just made him want to get back and do it again. "I'm sure guys are hungry and ready to start next season already because I know I am," Kevin said.

Unfortunately for Kevin and his teammates, the next season wouldn't come as soon as he hoped.

9
The Finals

THE 2011–12 NBA season was delayed due to a work stoppage, or "lockout," as owners and players negotiated over how to fairly split up the money the league earned. It was frustrating for everyone, especially Kevin and the Thunder, who were desperate to get back to chasing a championship.

During the lockout, the players were not allowed to enter team facilities. There were no practices or summer league. And by late October, there was no regular season.

Kevin always said he played basketball because

of his love of the game, not the money. He proved it that summer and fall when, with nothing else to do, he began showing up at parks and playing pick-up games on blacktop courts. It was like he was just a normal guy, a teenager again crashing the action at the King Dome in PG County, not someone who had led the NBA in scoring for three consecutive years.

When Kevin would arrive at public courts across the country, social media would start buzzing, and fans would flock to the park, running in from the surrounding neighborhoods for a chance to watch. Later, cell phone footage of Kevin draining threes or hammering home dunks would spring up on YouTube. Fans loved to see a guy play with passion and interact with people in a humble way, all while watching him dominate on the court.

Kevin's most famous streetball appearance came on August 1, 2011, when he walked onto the court at the famed Holcombe Rucker Park in Harlem, a neighborhood in New York City. Rucker Park has long been home to great players, and its summer leagues and tournament often attract former college players and upcoming high school stars as well as talented locals who never played organized ball. It puts a premium on trick dribbles, deep jumpers, and dunks, all while an announcer hypes up the fans. Often a DJ is there playing music. Rucker Park has been featured in numerous books and movies, including 2018's *Uncle Drew*, starring Kyrie Irving, Shaq, and other NBA greats.

On that night, Kevin tore it up, scoring sixty-six points. His performance included draining a number of wild three-pointers at the end. The crowd was so big it didn't just pack the bleachers that run alongside the park, it ringed the court, fans standing four or five deep and going crazy with each shot.

Recordings of the performance, complete with Kevin celebrating with fans who rushed the court at the end, have racked up tens of millions of views on YouTube. Not even an NBA lockout could stop Kevin from playing his game.

"Only thing I remember was that everybody ran on the court," Kevin said. "That's probably one of the best moments I've had so far in my life, playing at the mecca of basketball in New York City. It felt like everybody just swarmed me so quickly. It was just a fun moment for me and something I'm always going to remember."

A deal between the players and owners was eventually reached and the season began on Christmas

Day, around two months later than normal. There was only room for a sixty-six-game schedule, not the traditional eighty-two-game season. Kevin didn't waste any time. He scored thirty or more in each of the Thunder's first four games, all victories.

Kevin was named to his third consecutive All-Star game that year, although it was his first as a starter. He proved he deserved the honor by scoring thirty-six points and being named the game's MVP. "As a kid you dream of playing in an All-Star game, but to be MVP is another level," Kevin said. "I'm excited I got it."

One of the more interesting parts of the game was a stretch when Kevin and Russell were on the court together and taking turns scoring and making plays. Then at the other end of the court, Eastern Conference All-Stars LeBron James and Dwyane Wade would go right back at them by doing the same. The showdown was in an All-Star game, not a competition that truly mattered, but it was obvious what was going on. The Thunder and the Heat were staring each other down in case they met in June's NBA Finals.

"It's too early for that," Kevin said when asked about the Heat after the game.

OKC fans didn't think so—they were eyeing The Finals. Kevin averaged 28.0 points a game, Russ went for 23.6, and James Harden had 16.8 despite coming off the bench as a reserve. James was named the NBA's Sixth Man of the Year, which is awarded to the best player in the league who isn't a starter. Kevin was so good he finished second in voting for the league MVP, but was beaten out by LeBron.

Waiting for OKC in round one of the playoffs was Dallas, the defending champs who had ended the Thunder's season the year before. But this was a different Thunder team, one that was more experienced, better at balancing the scoring, and focused on doing the little things to win games.

Kevin wound up hitting a jumper with 1.5 seconds left to win Game 1 for OKC. It set the mood for the series and the Thunder went on to sweep the Mavs, 4–0. In the second round, Kevin hit late, go-ahead shots in Games 2 and 4 to lead OKC past the Los Angeles Lakers—the team that had eliminated them two seasons ago—four games to one.

That was two former nemeses down. The Thunder was no longer a team on the rise. They had risen.

As LeBron and the Heat rolled through the

Eastern Conference, OKC matched up with the San Antonio Spurs in the Western Conference Finals. This was a major test. Under Coach Gregg Popovich and behind stars such as Tim Duncan, Manu Ginobili, and Tony Parker, the Spurs would win five NBA championships. When the Spurs won the first two games on their home court, plenty of fans and media figured that experience would again win out and the Thunder were just still too young.

Back in Oklahoma for Game 3, the Thunder were determined not to get blown out of the playoffs. At a practice session, they talked about the pain and disappointment of the season before and how everything could change in a hurry. Then they went out and pounded the Spurs by twenty in Game 3 to make the series 2–1.

"We played harder," Kevin said after.

Whatever it was, the series flipped on a dime. In a Game 4 victory, Kevin scored thirty-six points and dished eight assists for another OKC victory. In Game 5, back in San Antonio, Kevin, Russ, and James all scored twenty or more to steal a game on the Spurs home court.

Now OKC was up 3–2, with a chance to close out San Antonio in Game 6. That's when Kevin came out with one of the best games of his career . . . a thirty-four-point, fourteen-rebound bit of brilliance to overcome a fifteen-point deficit to win the game and series and advance OKC to the NBA Finals.

At last, they'd made it onto the grand stage.

The Thunder would match up against a desperate Miami Heat team in The Finals. LeBron James, Dwyane Wade, and Chris Bosh had come together to form a so-called "Super Team" that was supposed to win multiple NBA titles. Yet in year one of the experiment, they fell short to Dallas. Many fans hated the idea of top free agents coming together like that and preferred a "homegrown" team such as OKC, where most of the star players had been drafted out of college.

The NBA Finals brings a lot of attention and a lot of media not just from all over America, but all over the world. Basketball is played everywhere and the NBA is popular internationally. So now, not only were there the local Oklahoma City writers and broadcasters covering the game, but so too were journalists from across America and even China, Brazil, South Korea, Australia, and Europe.

Kevin was pitched to fans as the anti-LeBron, a guy who quietly re-signed with OKC rather than test free agency. That wasn't fair to LeBron, though. He had played eight seasons with the Cleveland Cavaliers, the team that had drafted him, before going to Miami because he felt it was the best opportunity to win. Kevin tried to defend LeBron, who was a friend he had worked out with during the lockout. He also didn't want the discourse of the NBA Finals to turn into a KD vs. LeBron story, leaving the rest of their teammates to be ignored.

"Everybody is going to make the most out of the matchup of me versus LeBron, but it's the Thunder versus the Heat," Kevin said. "One guy versus another guy, it's not going to be a one-on-one matchup to win the series. It's going to be all about the team."

The other thing the media was focused on was youth versus experience. Kevin and Russ were still just twenty-three years old. James and Serge were only twenty-two. Meanwhile, LeBron was twenty-seven, Chris Bosh twenty-eight, and Dwyane was thirty. Could these kids from OKC really steal the title?

Kevin reflected back to his days growing up in PG County. "Of course everybody is going to say it's not our time, we're too young," he said. "But that's not the approach we ever want to take with anything. I learned that when I was a kid. My mom always told me when I was going against older guys, 'don't let your age be the reason why you don't succeed.'"

Game 1 of the NBA Finals was played in Oklahoma City, and in front of a wild crowd, the Thunder shocked the league by winning, 105–94. The Heat jumped out to an early lead, but OKC proved that despite their age, they weren't going to panic. Kevin scored thirty-six points, including seventeen in the fourth quarter to put the game away. And that was just part of his impact. While LeBron scored thirty, he missed thirteen of his twenty-four shots, mainly because of some suffocating defense by Kevin, who was showing everyone his complete game.

"We all know how well he is as a scorer," OKC coach Scott Brooks said. "He's led the league three years in a row in scoring. But he is a special player because he defends, and we are a good basketball team because we defend."

Up 1–0, the Thunder were flying high while the media focused on whether Miami's "Big Three" would once again fall short of the championship. Yet the Heat players were veterans, and if fans were panicking, they certainly weren't.

"This is one game," LeBron said. "We will make adjustments. This is going to be a long series."

LeBron would end up being both correct and incorrect. He was right about the Heat making adjustments. They never could stop Kevin, who averaged a magnificent 30.6 points a game in The Finals, but they were able to slow down the rest of the Thunder attack while making the critical plays needed to win. Miami had a fully built roster and an understanding of who needed to take the big shot at the right time. OKC just wasn't quite there.

What LeBron was wrong about was it being a long series. After losing game one, Miami won each of the next four to claim the championship, 4–1. Once the Heat got things cranked up, there was no stopping them. And for OKC—just like that, the dream was over.

"It hurts," Kevin said. "It hurts, man. We're all brothers on this team, and it just hurts to go out like this. We made it to The Finals, which was cool for us, but we didn't want to just make it there. Unfortunately we lost, so it's tough. It's tough, man."

After the last game, as confetti fell on the celebrating Heat players, Kevin walked off the court and down a hallway to the locker room. He was frustrated, tired, and spent, both physically and emotionally. He'd put everything into winning and it wasn't enough. That's when he saw his mother and father waiting for him. They hugged him and as he felt their support, he couldn't help but start crying. He wasn't afraid to show just how painful this was.

"I didn't think I would get that emotional," Kevin said. "It was a tough, tough game, tough series. My mom and my dad have been there from the beginning . . . win or lose, they're going to always be there for me. You know, I'm not going to just hug them because we won a game . . . They hurt like I hurt. That's what you want your parents to go through. It's tough for me, and I could tell in my mom's face and my dad's face, it was tough for them just to see us lose."

He was determined not to allow that to happen again.

10

Frustrations

JUST WORKING HARD isn't enough to win an NBA championship. Accomplishing it is very difficult. One player can't do it. Two's not enough, either. You need a complete team. That's what makes a championship so special.

For OKC, the job didn't get easier when in the summer of 2012, James Harden was traded to Houston.

It is difficult to understand now how the Thunder couldn't win the title with Kevin, Russ, and James. These days, all three are among the best players in the league. At the time, though, only Kevin was considered a top-five player. Besides, under the NBA salary cap, it was impossible for the Thunder to extend each of them the lucrative contract that they deserved. James, as the sixth man, was the one who got shipped out. The team thought they could overcome the loss. In truth, they were never quite the same.

James's departure didn't show during the 2012–13 regular season, when the Thunder went an impressive 60–22 and looked like title contenders again. Kevin produced his best season, averaging not just 28.1 points a game, but doing so with great accuracy. He shot 53.9 percent from the floor, 41.6 percent from three-point range, and 90.5 percent from the foul line. He was incredible.

The only other player to ever be that efficient and average over twenty-eight points a game? Larry Bird, the Hall of Famer whose game film and style Coach Brown made Kevin study way back when.

The playoffs began with the Thunder taking on James Harden and his new team, the Houston Rockets. OKC won, but Russ got injured and was lost for the rest of the playoffs. Now not having Harden showed. Kevin was the only difference maker still standing on OKC, and it was a big reason why, in the second round, Memphis beat them four games to one.

For Kevin, the early exit was frustrating. He felt like it was the NBA title or bust at this point. He didn't need scoring titles or All-Star games to show people he was great. He needed championship rings. He'd won a gold medal representing the United States at the 2012 Olympics (and would win another in 2016). It was a dream come true for nearly any person, but all that did was make him want an NBA title even more. Yet he kept coming up short.

"I've been second my whole life," Kevin told *Sports Illustrated* in 2013. "I was the second-best player in high school. I was the second pick in the draft. I've been second in MVP voting three times. I came in second in The Finals. I'm tired of being second. I'm not going to settle for it."

The Thunder went 59–23 in 2013–14. Kevin was brilliant, leading the league in scoring for the fourth time in five years (averaging 32.0 points per game). At one point during the season, he scored at least twenty-five points in forty-one consecutive games and OKC piled up the victories despite Russ missing a lot of time due to injury.

It was enough for one of Kevin's dreams to come true—he was voted the NBA's Most Valuable Player. The competition was a landslide with Kevin earning 119 of 125 first-place votes. LeBron came in second.

At the award ceremony, Kevin gave one of the most memorable, and emotional, acceptance speeches in league history. Rather than read some prepared remarks, he brought just a few notes and spoke from the heart about what winning the award meant to him. Mostly he thanked everyone who helped him along the way—coaches, teammates, mentors, friends, God, and so on.

He saved the best for his family, including his grandmother, his brother Tony, and his half-siblings from his father's later relationship, Rayvonne and Brianna Pratt. He took special time to speak about his dad and all they had been through.

"Dad, it's been an up-and-down road for all of us, but you've always been there supporting from afar, texting me Bible verses every single day, telling me you love me every single day," Kevin said. "I'm just glad you're part of this journey with us."

And then he got to his mother. Kevin had to fight through tears to express his thanks for all the sacrifices she'd made for him and his brother, Tony, who played college ball at Towson University in Maryland and had become a successful businessman.

"We wasn't supposed to be here," Kevin said. "You made us believe. You kept us off the street. You put clothes on our backs, food on the table. When you didn't eat, you made sure we ate. You went to sleep hungry. You sacrificed for us.

"You the real MVP."

The speech went viral. Even non-basketball fans were drawn into this great athlete weeping in appreciation of his mother, all while telling the quiet story of so many other single mothers and struggling young families. It was one more way that Kevin connected with fans on a personal level. "You the real MVP" became a catchphrase and Internet meme.

Unfortunately for Kevin, winning the MVP didn't help in the playoffs. The Thunder made it to the Western Conference Finals but lost 4–2 to the San Antonio Spurs, who would go on to beat Miami for the championship.

It got worse in 2014–15, when a foot injury caused Kevin's quest for a title to end early. Kevin played just twenty-seven games before having a series of surgeries to deal with recurring soreness.

While there was hope he could return quickly, things didn't heal as expected. OKC missed the playoffs without him. That Finals appearance three years prior was beginning to feel like ancient history.

The Thunder decided to reboot that offseason and fired Coach Scott Brooks. He was replaced by Billy Donovan, who had coached the University of Florida to two NCAA titles, and was considered a top offensive coach. Kevin was excited for the new approach and energy around the team. He felt like if he would be healthy, this could finally be the year.

Kevin was set to become a free agent again after the 2015–16 season. Unlike in the past, he declined to sign a new contract before the season that would've guaranteed a long-term stay in OKC. He loved the city, the fans, and his teammates, but he wanted to keep his options open. He was twenty-seven years old, with enough experience to know that it was in his best interest to see how everything played out before committing more of his prime years to a team with a brand-new coach that still hadn't won the title.

His possible departure became a huge story in the media and was a constant topic of conversation among fans on social media. Everyone had an opinion. Meanwhile, a number of other franchises were positioning themselves in case Kevin decided he wanted to leave the Thunder at the end of the season. Kevin just kept trying to deflect the attention. His priorities were simple: Win the title that year for OKC and then figure it out.

Accomplishing that goal was aided by the fact Kevin was healthy again. He averaged 28.2 points and 8.2 rebounds a game and OKC's regular season record was an impressive 55–27.

The Thunder cruised in the opening round of the playoffs, beating Dallas 4–1 before taking out San Antonio in six games in the next round to advance to the Western Conference Finals, where an imposing matchup waited—with the Golden State Warriors.

Behind stars Stephen Curry, Klay Thompson, and Draymond Green, the Warriors had become a league-wide sensation. They played an exciting, up-tempo style with a lot of three-pointers and dunks. Curry and Thompson were known as "the Splash Brothers" for the way their three-pointers hit the net. By that point, the pair were well on their way to establishing themselves as two of the greatest long-distance shooters in NBA history. The Warriors had won the NBA championship in 2014–15 and then came back in 2015–16 and won an NBA record seventy-three games—edging out the Michael Jordan–led 1995–96 Chicago Bulls team by one win.

The Warriors had lost fewer than ten games all season long. They were the hot franchise. They were the favorite.

They were everything OKC wanted to be . . . and everything they wanted to beat.

Game 1 was played at Golden State's Oracle Arena in Oakland, California, where the Warriors almost never lost. The Thunder didn't care. They stunned the Warriors 108–102 mostly thanks to balanced scoring and getting key stops at the end of the game.

"I mean, you hear it all the time," Kevin said. "Defense wins."

Golden State took Game 2, but when the series shifted back to Oklahoma City, the Thunder and their rabid fans felt like an opportunity was at hand. In Game 3, Kevin scored thirty-three, Russ scored thirty, and OKC absolutely crushed the Warriors 133–105. In the third quarter, the Thunder lead hit forty points and they could do no wrong. Golden State, which rarely lost at all and even more rarely was manhandled like this, couldn't do anything right.

"We got our butts kicked," Golden State coach Steve Kerr said.

Then, in Game 4, the Warriors got them kicked again. Kevin had twenty-six and Russ had thirty-six as OKC won 118–94. It was the second consecutive game that the Thunder scored seventy-two points in the first half to put Golden State in a hole. OKC was playing fast and confidently, while defensively they were able to harass the usually reliable Steph Curry into missed shots and turnovers.

The Thunder now led the series 3–1. It needed just one more victory, with three chances to do it, to advance to the NBA Finals. Kevin and his teammates knew that if they could defeat mighty Golden State, then they could certainly win the NBA championship. This was the opportunity they had been working toward for years.

They also were told that in the history of the NBA, just nine teams had ever come back from a 3–1 deficit and won the series. Usually if you get up 3–1, you win; not that OKC could count on anything. Golden State certainly wasn't scared.

"Well, we are the defending champs," Coach Steve Kerr said. "Most teams that are down 3–1 in the Conference Finals . . . I'm guessing most of them weren't the defending champs. We feel very confident. We've got potentially three games, two of them at home."

Kevin did all he could in Game 5 to end the series right then and there. In an electric offensive performance, he scored forty. But the Warriors hadn't won all those games by accident. Steph Curry finished with thirty-one points, and Klay Thompson had twenty-seven, and Golden State rode its home crowd's energy to a 120–111 victory.

Meanwhile, while Kevin and Russ combined for seventy-one points, the rest of the Thunder were held in check. It was a sign of how little depth the Thunder now had. Just six players got significant minutes. They missed James Harden desperately.

Still, OKC kept their heads up going into Game 6, excited to return to their home court and play in front of their home fans. They'd dominated the first two games played there and this would be the ideal time to eliminate the Warriors. No one wanted to have to travel back to California for a Game 7.

With five minutes left in the fourth quarter, OKC led 96–89. Kevin had just hit a jump shot for his twenty-eighth and twenty-ninth points of the night. Despite his high point total, he hadn't played that well offensively, and would finish the game having missed twenty-one of his thirty-one shots.

His effort was undeniable, though. Even if his shots weren't falling, he was going to leave everything out on the court. Now the Thunder were up seven and noise was pulsating from their crowd.

They kept pushing and pushing. But so too did Golden State.

The teams exchanged free throws and then Curry drained a big-time three to cut the Thunder's lead to 97–96. Two Russ free throws got it back to 99–96, but then Curry hit another three and it was tied.

Coach Donovan called time-out and the once raucous arena was suddenly silent. Everyone feared that the Warriors couldn't be stopped.

With just over two minutes left, the game was tied at 101. At that critical moment, Russ had a turnover, and when the Warriors got back on offense, Klay hit a three for the Warriors. Golden State led 104–101. Then Kevin tried to rally his team back with a long jumper, but his shot didn't fall.

After the miss, Steph hit another basket, and just like that, Golden State put some more distance between itself and OKC, extending its lead to 106–101. The Thunder scrambled, but Russ had a couple turnovers before Klay iced it with some free throws, giving him forty-one clutch points on the night.

In a matter of minutes, the lead had disappeared—in both the game and the series. The Warriors won 108–101 and the Western Conference Finals were knotted at three games apiece.

The loss was a missed opportunity and Kevin knew it. The chance had been there, a spot in the championship mere minutes away, yet he'd failed to get the extra basket that would've altered the final moments of the game. He was asked if he had pressed and put too much pressure on himself because he was simply desperate to win.

"I think it's okay to want it so much," Kevin said. "I think sometimes you want to calm down a bit because you want something so bad. It's difficult to really talk about because it's something that I've been feeling. It's like you've been dreaming about this moment since you were a kid. You've been wanting this moment since you were a kid . . . I think that it's okay to want it so bad. But at the same time, I've just got to relax a bit."

Game 7 was back in Oakland and, despite playing on their opponents' home court, OKC actually led by six at the half. Then late in the third quarter, the

Warriors put together a 12–2 run and never trailed again. The Thunder managed to inch closer late in the game, but they still lost 96–88.

Kevin scored twenty-seven, but no one else on the team topped twenty. Meanwhile the dual threat of Curry (thirty-six points) and Thompson (twenty-one points) proved to be too much for the Thunder to handle. The Warriors would eventually lose to the Cleveland Cavaliers, again led by LeBron James, who had recently returned from the Miami Heat.

OKC's loss was a crushing blow for Kevin, who felt just as dejected as he had been when OKC lost in the NBA Finals to the Heat.

"You know, it hurts losing," Kevin said. "It hurts losing, especially being up three games to one . . . We fought. Everybody fought hard every single minute they were on the court."

The agony of defeat upon him, Kevin now had a decision to make . . . should he stay in Oklahoma City and try for a championship again? Or seek out a fresh start—and a fresh shot at the title—on a new team?

11

Decisions

WITH FREE AGENCY upon him, Kevin was asked what he was looking for in a team.

"Just being around great people, being in a great basketball environment—that's the two most important things for me," Kevin said. "That's all I really care about. Who I'm going to be doing life with every single day, who I'm going to be playing basketball with every day."

What he left unsaid was that he wanted to win. The forever runner-up wanted a championship and he wasn't sure it would ever come in OKC. Much like how LeBron James had to leave Cleveland for Miami to win his first two titles, Kevin began to think there was greener grass somewhere else.

He was also a little older now. He would turn twenty-eight before the 2016–17 season, and with age had come maturity and perspective. He truly didn't care about being considered the star of the team, or the leading scorer, or being the highest paid. While OKC could give him the most money because of league salary rules, Kevin knew he'd be paid well wherever he went. Besides, in 2014, he'd signed a $300 million deal with Nike. He had more money than he could ever spend.

There was one thing that no amount of money could buy—an NBA championship.

With Kevin potentially available, the NBA went into full recruitment mode. It felt like every team wanted him. It was so overwhelming that Kevin narrowed his list down to just six teams—the San Antonio Spurs, Boston Celtics, Miami Heat, Los Angeles Clippers, his recent foe the Golden State Warriors, and, of course, Oklahoma City. He then tried to seek out some peace and quiet by renting a mansion for ten days in the exclusive beach area of New York known as the Hamptons. His dad and agent joined him out there to meet with representatives from most of the teams.

As the team entourages arrived, they pitched Kevin on why he should sign with them, each offering different visions. San Antonio tried to sell him on a culture of winning championships—something the Spurs had learned across years and championships—and its great coach, Gregg Popovich. The Clippers pitched an up-and-coming franchise and life in sunny Los Angeles. Miami, now in need of elite talent after losing LeBron to the Cavs, offered both a winning tradition and the beach.

Everyone had an angle. The Boston Celtics didn't just send their coach, general manager, and a few of their players to the meeting. Kevin was stunned when the group pulled up to his house in a limousine and out stepped . . . Tom Brady, the star quarterback of the New England Patriots.

Kevin couldn't believe it. He was a huge football fan and had watched every Super Bowl Tom had ever played for the Patriots, whose home stadium is just outside of Boston. Tom was one of the greatest, and most accomplished, athletes in the world and now he was explaining to Kevin how wonderfully Boston fans treat their star athletes.

It was quite a presentation and Kevin appreciated Tom taking the time out of his busy life to recruit him to the Celtics. It almost worked.

"I was ready to just say, 'all right, let's go. I'm ready to go,' seeing Tom Brady there," Durant said. "Seeing someone so successful at his craft, and just a great ambassador for the game of football and the city of Boston. It was great to be in the presence of greatness."

That said, Kevin wasn't looking for a new friend or the love from fans that Tom talked about. He was looking for an NBA championship. As cool as it was for Tom to come all the way to the Hamptons to see him, this was a basketball decision.

"I knew I couldn't let [Tom] distract me," Kevin said.

The team he most wanted to hear from was Golden State. While the Warriors couldn't bring a Super Bowl hero with them, they didn't disappoint.

Along with Coach Steve Kerr and management, four players made the trip . . . Steph Curry, Klay Thompson, Draymond Green, and Andre Iguodala. It was only a few weeks since the Warriors had stormed back from 3–1 to break Kevin's heart, but now they had taken time out of their brief offseason to fly across the country to pitch him on joining them to win titles. They wanted Kevin to know that despite all the group had accomplished, they needed him to keep it up.

"Strength in Numbers," was their slogan. Steph said he didn't care who was the biggest star on the team, he just wanted to win. That was exactly what Kevin had been saying. Soon the players were sitting there, like a bunch of friends, wondering just how many titles they could all win together . . . if Kevin was willing to sign with Golden State.

"I was shocked that those four guys came to meet me," Kevin said. "The team won seventy-three games and a championship [the year] before. I didn't think they would be interested in a player like me because they've had so much success. But to see them together, they all walked in and it looked like they were holding hands. It was just a family. I could tell they enjoyed being around each other, and like I said, that was something I couldn't ignore."

While Oklahoma City was familiar and comfortable and the safest decision, Kevin kept asking himself what was the best decision in terms of basketball. That is what ultimately gave Golden State the edge. Winning a title was his sole focus. He wasn't married. (He'd been engaged for a stretch to WNBA player Monica Wright, who grew up in PG County as well, but they broke it off.) He had no children. His life was hoops.

His only fear at that point was the public backlash. Once word broke that the Warriors were one of the finalists in the Kevin Durant free agency sweepstakes, fans complained that Kevin was just giving up and taking the easy road to a title. A real fighter, they argued, would stay in Oklahoma, alongside Russell Westbrook, and try to beat Golden State, not join them. Others complained about the potential of Kevin and the Warriors forming another "Super Team," fearing the NBA would be boring over the next few years because Golden State would surely dominate.

Kevin saw it differently. He was joining excellence, yes, but why was that a bad thing? He'd worked hard through the years to become the type of player that Golden State wanted. What was wrong with taking advantage of that? In college basketball, many of the best players often sign with the same team. Why not in the NBA? In every profession, people want to be surrounded by the best.

If anything, it was a somewhat humble move for a player of Kevin's magnitude to join a team that already had a bigger name in Steph, rather than choose a team where he'd be the undisputed star and bask in all of the attention. Stardom was what Tom Brady had tried to sell him on in Boston. Instead, Kevin was willing to be the second or even third most popular player on his team.

Finally, over the July Fourth weekend, Kevin believed he had reached a decision. He'd sat up late through the night with his dad and agent going through the pros and cons of each team. His destination was clear, but he knew it would disappoint a lot of people. "The toughest day of my life," he called it.

"I was just torn, and I told them I wanted to sleep on it," Kevin said. "When I woke up [at] about seven in the morning, I walked in their rooms. They were all asleep. I woke them up."

His mind was made.

"I want to go to the Warriors," he said.

With his choice made, Kevin did the proper thing and called the Thunder to tell them that after nine years with the franchise (one in Seattle and eight in OKC), he was leaving.

"That call to Oklahoma City was the hardest thing I've ever had to do in my life," Kevin said. "Tears were shed. But this is a new journey for me, testing the unknown, and I trusted it. I trusted my gut. I trusted my instincts. It's the unpopular decision, but I can live with it."

He later called and texted his teammates, coaches, and support staff. It wasn't easy, especially for Russell Westbrook.

"I talked to him," Kevin said. "It's tough. Obviously we were teammates for so long and I had a lot of great memories. I'm sure he wasn't happy about the decision, but he respected it as my friend . . . But like I said, I wanted a new chapter in my life . . . I'm sure they won't be the same, but I still wanted to go out there and leave with some class and some dignity, but hopefully I did. Hopefully he understands."

As for the fans who were upset he joined an already great team, he said he felt bad. That was especially true for the Thunder fans, who took to social media and talk radio to express their frustrations. He was no longer beloved. Some even burned their KD jerseys. Kevin tried to brush it aside.

"We live in this superhero comic book world where either you're a villain or you're a superhero," Kevin said. "I know I haven't changed as a person."

This was his life. This was his decision. And this was his future.

He was California-bound.

12

Golden

THROUGHOUT HIS CAREER, Kevin had been considered a likeable player, even by fans of other teams. They might've groaned when he hit game-winning shots against their favorite club or screamed to distract him during critical free-throw attempts, but they'd respected him.

It wasn't just his unique game that made him worthy of their admiration—this near seven-footer bringing the ball up the court and hitting long three-pointers. It was also the way he carried himself. The humble way that he talked to the media.

His devotion to his faith and his family. The respect he showed opponents.

He seemed like a good guy who was really good at basketball.

In many ways, Stephen Curry (not to mention Klay Thompson) was viewed in a similar light. Kevin and Steph were among the most popular athletes on earth, as jersey sales and Instagram follower statistics proved. When they played on the road, the arenas were always sold out, fans coming to see them in action, if not root them on.

Then Steph and KD and Klay all joined together. And suddenly, just like that, they were villains.

Once the season started, they were booed on the road by opposing fans (although plenty of Warriors supporters in the house would cheer as well). Fans openly rooted for any team other than Golden State to win it all. For the first time in Kevin's life, he received truly negative attention. He had to shrug it off. He knew there was no value in allowing other people's opinions to bother him.

"I can't control that," Kevin said. "All I can control is how I come to work every single day and what I do to help this team win. I knew that was a part of this whole deal. That's just the life we live . . . I can't really worry about the outside noise."

It wasn't easy. At times Kevin would get frustrated with media questions. Occasionally, Kevin would respond to social media haters and try to defend himself. He was even caught making extra accounts, which were designed to be secret, just for friends and family to follow, but then used them to argue with critics.

Almost everyone struggles with social media. While Kevin was teased for having second and third accounts, it actually showed him to be a regular person. Even someone who appears to have everything—fame, money, success—can find attacks on social media to be troubling and painful. It isn't easy to shake it off.

For Kevin and the rest of the Warriors, the key was just focusing on what they could control—basketball. It's always better to listen to the many people cheering or supporting you than the few who are trying to tear you down. And when it came to basketball, Golden State was as great as everyone expected with so many offensive weapons.

In the first quarter of the first game of Golden State's 2016–17 season, Kevin Durant scored nine points and Stephen Curry scored seven. The Warriors would lose to San Antonio that night, but it hardly mattered. In the end Kevin had twenty-nine and

Steph twenty-seven and it was clear to the NBA that the two would complement each other on the court.

That's how the season would go. When Steph wasn't hitting shots, Kevin or Klay was. When Kevin wasn't, Steph or Klay was. Or Draymond Green. Or Andre Iguodala. Or they would just all concentrate on locking it down on defense.

The Warriors played the game like a symphony, beautiful and victorious almost every single night. Gone were the days of lacking depth in OKC or having just Russ to bail him out. Kevin was having fun. The Warriors didn't just rack up victory after victory; they played the game with joy, no matter what opposing fans thought.

"We're all different and unique and bring things to the table that confuses the defense," Kevin said. "We bring pressure to the defense. We all do it to-gether . . . we've loved this game our whole lives."

Long win streaks were peeled off. Points piled up. Golden State scored over 130 points in five different games and even beat Indiana 142–106. Klay caught fire that night and scored sixty. Kevin was more than content with passing his teammate the ball and watching the show. That's how it had to be on a team with so many future Hall of Fame players.

Kevin would average 25.1 points a game that year, his lowest since his rookie season in Seattle. He was no longer a contender for highest in the league. He didn't care. He also shot a career high 60.8 percent from the floor (up from 45.1 percent during his rookie year in Seattle).

The Warriors stars took turns being the focus of the offense. Kevin had fourteen games of scoring more than thirty. He even put up forty points in a highly anticipated and emotional game against his old team, Oklahoma City. As the Warriors racked up a 67–15 record, it was clear this was the best, truest team Kevin had ever played for. The players were selfless. They didn't care about stats. They didn't care about media attention. They only cared about winning.

The year before Kevin arrived, the Warriors won seventy-three games but were upset in the NBA Finals by LeBron, Kyrie Irving, and the Cleveland Cavaliers. There was a sense that the Golden State players had run out of energy against the Cavs, so in 2016–17 Coach Steve Kerr took time to limit minutes and make sure everyone was fresh for the playoffs. It worked, and the Warriors were on another level come the postseason.

They swept Portland in the first round. They swept Utah in the second round. They swept San Antonio in the Western Conference Finals. Twelve games up, twelve victories. The games weren't even very close. Golden State won by an average of 16.3 points a game and only twice was the margin in single digits. Fans and media began wondering if the Warriors could be the first team to have a perfect postseason and go 16–0 to win the championship.

If anything, the easy victories were causing the Warriors to get *too* little credit. Fans just pointed to the roster and said, "Look how many great players they have." But San Antonio coach Gregg Popovich, who has won five NBA titles and is one of the greatest coaches in basketball history, made a point to correct that after the Warriors overwhelmed the Spurs.

This wasn't just talented players. It was a real team. Just saying "they're supposed to win" bothered him.

"That is disrespectful to them in my book," Coach Popovich said. "They're way, way more than just their talent . . . they're really talented. But that's not the whole equation. That's not everything that describes them. This is, you know, maybe the best defensive team in the league on top of everything. So they don't just play with talent. They execute at the defensive end of the floor. On offense, no team is more unselfish finding the open man and that sort of thing. They get credit for that. Coaches are always trying to get their team to do that."

LeBron and the Cavaliers awaited in The Finals. The Warriors wanted revenge, mostly for their defeat the year before. For Kevin, it was his first chance at LeBron in The Finals since 2012, when his young Thunder team had been beaten by the Miami Heat. By now they were considered two of the three best players in the NBA (along with Steph Curry). While Steph was great and a two-time MVP, Kevin and LeBron played similar games—they could line up at every position, defend nearly any opposing player, and both score from deep or down on the block.

It's part of what made that epic Game 3 shot, as described in the opening chapter, so great. It came directly over LeBron James. That's how the series went, though—Golden State was just a little too good and too deep for Cleveland. The Cavs' only success came in Game 4, when they sprung the upset and ruined the Warriors' chance to go a perfect 16–0 record in the playoffs. Golden State had to settle for 16–1 when they won the title in Game 5.

That was fine with Kevin. He was a champion at last and The Finals MVP.

Kevin scored thirty-nine points in the final game of the series to help Golden State win, 129–120. In the final minute, it was clear the Warriors were going to win, and Kevin was so overcome with emotion, he could barely even play.

"It was fifty-five seconds left, and I went over to [the] half-court line and I bent down, and I'm like, 'is this really happening?'" Kevin said later, laughing. "And Draymond was like, 'keep playing to the end. We have like fifty seconds left.'"

"It feels amazing to win a championship with these guys," Kevin said. ". . . Man, you've got to want to sacrifice. You've got to want to put your teammates in front of yourself sometimes."

It felt just as amazing when Golden State did it again the following year. Once again, the victim in The Finals was Cleveland, only this time the Warriors were able to complete the sweep. And once again, Kevin hit a critical Game 3 three-pointer—a final-minute basket dubbed the "déjà vu dagger"—to give the Warriors a commanding lead. For the second consecutive year, he earned Finals MVP honors.

With two titles in two years, it was clear Kevin had made the right choice basketball-wise. He also continued to impact the world outside of the game.

He founded The Kevin Durant Charity Foundation and poured his energy, and his money, into helping kids who had grown up in similar environments as he had. The projects are varied—from building quality basketball courts in cities across the world, including in China, Germany, and India, to fighting youth homelessness in America. And, of course, he's made a huge commitment to the Seat Pleasant Activity Center, which now bears his name, and where Kevin funds a number of youth teams.

His biggest endeavor, though, is a $10 million grant to bring the College Track program to students in Prince George's County. College Track is a comprehensive system that helps underprivileged high school students prepare, reach, afford, and eventually graduate from college. It's based out of The Durant Center, which was constructed in PG to serve as a home for the students.

"This is a realization of a dream of mine," Kevin

said. "To come back home and positively impact the lives of kids who share the ambitions I've always had."

● ● ●

As they had the year before, Kevin and the Warriors appeared to be enjoying similar success during the 2018–19 season. They stormed into the playoffs as a favorite to win the championship. They beat the Los Angeles Clippers in round one to set up a series against the Houston Rockets, who had emerged of late as the Warriors' chief threat. Golden State had needed seven games (including rallying from a 3–2 deficit) the year prior to beat the Rockets, which were led by Kevin's old OKC teammate James Harden.

The two teams split the first four contests, increasing the importance of Game 5. Kevin had twenty-two points and the Warriors led by three when late in the third quarter, after hitting a jump shot, he began running back down the court and felt his right calf give out. He suddenly couldn't move. Play stopped and he hobbled off the court as Oracle Arena fell into a hush.

It was soon determined he had strained his right calf and was out of the rest of the game. The Warriors lived up to their motto—"Strength in

Numbers"—and Steph and Klay won the Warriors the game and eventually the series, 4–2. Concern was high, though. The question on everyone's mind was: Could Golden State win a championship without Kevin?

They had enough talent in their arsenal to sweep Portland in the Western Conference Finals as Kevin rehabbed, but an excellent Toronto team awaited in The Finals. The Raptors were deep and talented and featured star Kawhi Leonard. Golden State struggled to score without Kevin as an option. Toronto won three of the first four games, pushing the Warriors to the brink.

Kevin had been working out relentlessly in an effort to return in time to help his teammates in The Finals. He felt helpless sitting and watching. As always, he wanted to be on the court, competing for a championship—in this case, a potential three-peat for the Warriors.

Finally, before Game 5, he felt ready to play. A team of Golden State doctors felt he could do it. General Manager Bob Myers gave the blessing and Kevin returned to the court looking to save the series, the season, and the championship.

Part of the way through the second quarter,

everything was working as planned. Kevin scored eleven points, grabbed two rebounds, blocked a shot, and looked like his old self. The Warriors led by five. Golden State's centerpiece had returned and another championship seemed possible.

Then, in an instant, injury struck again.

Kevin tried to cross over another old OKC teammate, Serge Ibaka, and get to the basket when his right leg failed again. Only this time it was worse. He fell to the court and couldn't move. He was eventually lifted up and limped off the court.

He'd ruptured his Achilles tendon, which sits just above the heel. It was a devastating injury, one that not just ended Kevin's Finals run, but can take six to twelve months to heal. Suddenly his 2019–2020 season was in jeopardy.

"I'm hurting deep in my soul," Kevin said on social media.

Golden State, behind a big effort by Steph, was able to hold off Toronto in Game 5, but eventually the Raptors won the Championship in Game 6 after Klay sustained a major injury to his knee. It was a terrible, horrible week for Golden State, filled with losses and injuries.

After Kevin went down, Bob Myers, the Warriors

general manager, addressed the media and openly cried when announcing the injury to the player he'd signed three years prior and had come to love.

"He's one of the most misunderstood people," Myers said. "He's a good teammate. He's a good person. It's not fair . . . I know Kevin takes a lot of hits sometimes, but he just wants to play basketball. And right now, he can't. Basketball has gotten him through his life . . . I don't know that we can all understand how much it means to him. He just wants to play basketball with his teammates and compete."

At the time, Myers didn't know that the injury and loss in The Finals would mark the bitter end to Kevin's career in Golden State. Kevin was again a free agent following the season, and a few weeks later he announced on Instagram that he was signing a four-year, $164 million contract with the Brooklyn Nets. There, he would join old rival Kyrie Irving in an effort to build a title contender in New York City.

The decision rocked the NBA. Many fans thought he should stay in Golden State and try to win more titles with Steph, Draymond, and Klay. The Warriors felt that despite the injuries to Kevin and Klay, they were still contenders. Golden State actually offered him more money than Brooklyn, but that didn't matter to Kevin. His decisions had never been about money. Others thought that if he was going to go to the East Coast, he should choose the New York Knicks, which play in Madison Square Garden in Manhattan. The franchise had spent two seasons clearing salary cap space in the hopes of signing both Kevin and Kyrie.

Instead Kevin chose the Nets, a franchise that had never won an NBA championship and with far fewer fans than the Knicks. Kevin actually found that lack of history and popularity appealing. The chance to join an up-and-coming team that was hungry to win a title felt like the old days in OKC. He wanted that challenge again.

Kevin's talent, star-power, and proven ability to win championships were enough for the Nets to sign him even though he faced a lengthy rehab of his Achilles and no one could be certain if he would ever truly return to top form as he entered his early thirties. Of course, with Kevin's work ethic and drive, there was little question that he would do everything he could to return to peak form.

There was one other big change, his number. Kevin would wear number 7 in Brooklyn rather than 35, the number he'd chosen all those years ago to honor Coach Craig. In making the change, Kevin wasn't forgetting his old friend or those childhood days spent dreaming of becoming a superstar. He just felt like it was time for a fresh start in every way.

"[The number] 35 was chosen in honor of someone very near and dear to me," Kevin said. "I will always honor him and honor the number 35. But as I start this new chapter in my basketball life, the number I'll be wearing on my back is the number 7."

Once again, the one-of-a-kind Kevin Durant was reinventing himself, blazing his own trail unconcerned about what others thought he should do. In Brooklyn, he was betting on himself and betting that he would find a way to thrill the basketball world with his play.

He had reason to be confident. It was a bet, after all, that time and time again had come true.

Instant
Replay

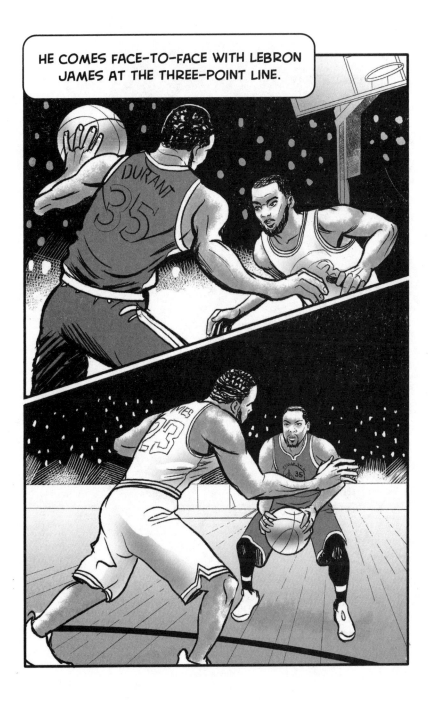

KEVIN ATTEMPTS A THREE-POINTER.

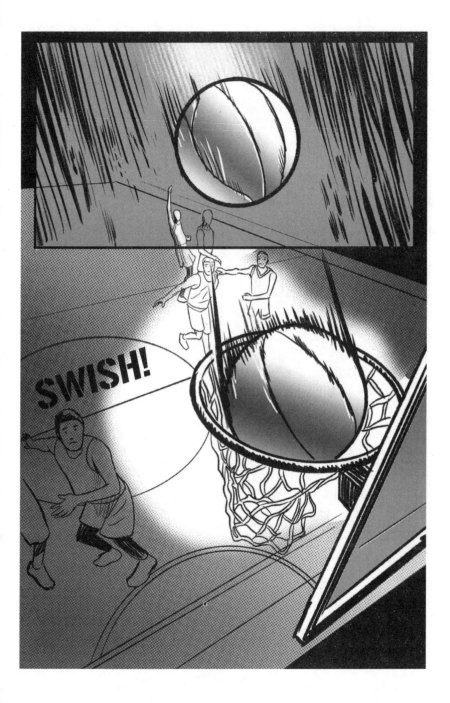

The Nonstop Sports Action Continues!

Here's an excerpt of
EPIC ATHLETES
LEBRON JAMES

GAME 7
FINALS 2016
CLE   GS
89   89
4th   1:55

1

The Block

Each and every fan, nearly twenty thousand in total, was on their feet inside Oracle Arena in Oakland, California. Standing in front of their seats. Standing on their seats. Standing in the aisles. They were too nervous to sit, after all.

With two minutes left in Game 7 of the 2016 NBA Finals, the Cleveland Cavaliers and the Golden State Warriors were tied 89–89. In addition to the twenty thousand in attendance, there were 44.5 million people tuned in to their televisions watching across America, and many millions more around the world.

While all those people were watching, LeBron James was searching—searching for a way to impact the game and seize a championship because he suddenly couldn't hit a jump shot. During the biggest moment of the biggest series, a series in which he'd averaged almost thirty points a game, LeBron couldn't make a basket.

In the final five minutes of the game, he missed from twenty-two feet, he missed from thirteen feet, he missed from two feet. He wasn't alone. The pressure was impacting everyone; the best players in the world were struggling with the intensity of the moment. LeBron's teammate Kyrie Irving had clanked a shot. So had fellow Cavalier Kevin Love. For the Warriors, Steph Curry had missed; so had Klay Thompson, Draymond Green, and Andre Iguodala.

Cleveland and Golden State had been battling for more than two and a half hours on this Father's Day. They had been going back and forth over nearly two weeks of this epic June championship clash. The action had been so even that not only was The Finals tied at three games apiece, and not only was this decisive game tied at 89, but at that very moment, each team had scored 699 cumulative points in the series. Everything was deadlocked.

Something had to give, though. There could only be one champion.

For LeBron, losing wasn't an option. He'd come too far to get to this point, to have this opportunity. He knew it meant too much to everyone not just back in Cleveland, but in all of Ohio, including the city of Akron, where he had grown up with a single mother and been a highly publicized star athlete since he was a kid.

He'd started his career with the Cavaliers in 2003 as the number one overall draft pick directly out of high school. He'd been crowned a basketball king before he ever stepped on a National Basketball Association (NBA) court and, by the age of eighteen, he'd already drawn comparisons to the legendary Michael Jordan, considered by many the greatest player of all time. But after seven seasons, even as he developed into the best player in the NBA, he couldn't win a championship. So, he left for Miami as a free agent.

Doing so angered fans back home in Ohio. They burned his jersey and cursed his name. They felt betrayed as he won two titles with the Miami Heat. Those should have been Cleveland's championships, they thought. Those should have been their victory parades, they complained.

LeBron didn't just win in Miami—more importantly, he learned *how* to win. He came to understand how it takes more than just scoring a lot of points and grabbing a lot of rebounds to become a champion. Winning requires sacrifice, teamwork, communication, and a mentality of doing whatever it takes—anything at all—to win, especially when you're losing.

It was a lesson he admits he didn't fully understand during his younger days with the Cavs. He said his four-year stretch in Miami was like "going off to college."

Older, wiser, and even more talented, he returned to Cleveland for the 2014–15 season, reigniting a love affair between himself and the fans in Northeast Ohio. He came back for one reason: to deliver that long-awaited championship to Cleveland. None of the city's three major professional sports teams had won a championship since 1964, when the Browns managed to win the National Football League title. By 2016, you needed to be well over the age of fifty to even remember it.

LeBron wanted to end that drought, or, as fans jokingly called it, the "curse." Cleveland is a blue-collar city of around 385,000 people and sits on Lake Erie. It is home to heavy industry, a major shipping port, and harsh winters. The city and its residents know what it's like to struggle. Unemployment. Crime. Poverty. Even jokes about its existence. In fact, back in 1969, the Cuyahoga River, which runs through the city, was so polluted with oil that it caught fire—literal burning water—and attracted insults and cracks from around America. Cleveland was dubbed the Mistake by the Lake.

The area wasn't a mistake for LeBron, though. It was simply home. Akron sits just over thirty miles to the south, almost a twin city for Cleveland, although smaller and poorer. And LeBron knew about overcoming the odds, about not accepting what others thought possible for you.

He was raised by a single teen mother, Gloria. His father was never around. His family was poor, accepting welfare to help buy food when his mom couldn't find work. They often couldn't afford to pay their rent, and were forced to move apartments in the city's toughest neighborhoods every few months before getting kicked out again. Sometimes, with nowhere else to go, they wound up sleeping on one of Gloria's friends' couches. All of LeBron's clothes and possessions fit into a single backpack. This was before he ever played organized sports or anyone saw him as a future NBA star.

In the fourth grade, LeBron was stuck living on

the other side of Akron from his elementary school. His mother didn't have a car, so it was a true struggle for him to find a ride to school in the mornings. He missed eighty-three days that year and was at risk of dropping out altogether even though he was just ten years old.

From that hopeless place, he rose.

And so regardless of how the outside world saw Northeast Ohio, LeBron knew this place. Yes, he knew the challenges. He also knew the positives, the success stories. He knew the good people in the community, the coaches and teachers who helped him and so many others. He knew his hometown's good times and happy stories, and the gorgeous summer sunsets. Mostly, he knew what a championship title, at last, would mean to his community.

In June of 2015, in his first season back in Cleveland, he led the Cavs to The Finals against Golden State. Injuries to star teammates Kyrie Irving and Kevin Love doomed them, though. The Warriors won four games to Cleveland's two. Now, twelve months later, it was a rematch.

Everyone on the Cavaliers was healthy and ready to prove they could be champions. It wouldn't be easy. Golden State had won a record seventy-three regular-season games and was considered possibly the greatest team in NBA history. Beating Curry, Thompson, and the rest of the Warriors felt at times like an impossible task. They had too many offensive weapons. Defensively they played with heart and toughness. When Golden State took a 3–1 series lead, many people wrote off Cleveland. After all, no team had ever come back from a 3–1 deficit in the NBA Finals, let alone against a seventy-three-victory defending champion set to play two of the three final games at home.

LeBron didn't care about the odds. His motto was about taking everything one possession at a time. In Game 5, facing elimination on the road in Oakland, both LeBron and Kyrie scored forty-one points and Cleveland stunned Golden State, 112–97. Then back in Cleveland for Game 6, LeBron again scored forty-one points, along with dishing eleven assists, as the Cavs won 115–101 to force Game 7.

Despite not being able to finish off the series quickly, Golden State still had confidence heading into Game 7. They still believed they were the best team, especially playing in front of their own fans, who were making a deafening noise cheering them on. Tied at 89, the game—and the championship—was still there for the taking.

Hungry for More EPIC ATHLETES? Look Out for These Superstar Biographies, in Stores Now!